All Clear! Advanced

Idioms and Pronunciation in Context

Helen Kalkstein Fragiadakis

Contra Costa College
San Pablo, California

Heinle & Heinle Publishers
ITP An International Thomson Publishing Company

Pacific Grove • Albany • Bonn • Boston • Cincinnati • Detroit • London • Madrid • Melbourne
Mexico City • New York • Paris • San Francisco • Tokyo • Toronto • Washington

The Publication of All Clear! Advanced was directed by the members of the Newbury House Publishing Team at Heinle & Heinle:

Erik Gundersen, Editorial Director
Bruno R. Paul, Market Development Director
Kristin Thalheimer, Production Services Coordinator
Stanely J. Galek, Vice President and Publisher

Also participating in the publication of this program were:

Production Editor: Margellen Eschmann Killeen
Project Manager: Margaret Cleveland
Manufacturing Coordinator: Mary Beth Hennebury
Interior Line Artist: Brian Orr
Interior Text Designer: Carol H. Rose
Maryellen Eschmann Killeen, Production Editor
Cover Artist and Designer: Matthew Murphy and Gina Petti, Rotunda Design

LIBRARY OF CONGRESS CATALOGING-IN-PUBLICATION DATA

Fragiadakis, Helen Kalkstein.
  All Clear! Advanced: Idioms and pronunciation in context/ Helen Kalkstein Fragiadakis
     p.   cm.
  Includes index.
  ISBN 0-8384-4721-X
  1. English language—Textbooks for foreign speakers. 2. English language—Pronunciation.
3. English language—Idioms. I. Title.
PE1128.F63 1996
428.2'4–dc20   96-30941
                                                             CIP

Heinle & Heinle Publishers/A Division of International Thomson Publishing, Inc.

Manufactured in the United States of America

ISB 0-8 384-4721-X

10 9 8 7 6 5 4 3 2 1

Thank You

The author and publisher would like to thank the following individuals who offered may helpful insights and ideas during the planning for and development of *All Clear! Advanced:*

Kathleen Ann Berry, *University of California, Berkeley Extension*

Michele Bowman, *University of South Florida*

Glenda Bro, *Mt. San Antonio College (California)*

P. Charles Brown, *Concordia University (Montreal)*

Mary Ashley Hayes, *University of South Florida*

Karli Kelber, *New York University & LaGuardia Community College*

Tamara Lovell, *Cornell University*

Anne Ludwig, *University of Nebraska at Omaha*

Martha Lynch, *Mills College (California)*

Kathleen O'Hanlon, *University of North Texas*

Marta Pitt, *Lindsey Hopkins Technical Education Center (Miami)*

Jody Stern, *University of California, San Diego Extension*

Melva Underbakke, *University of South Florida*

Wendy Vicens, *Arizona State University*

Colleen Weldele, *Palomar College (California)*

Sharman Yoffie, *Long Island University, Brooklyn Campus*

Contents

Lesson 1: At a Party—
Taking the Initiative   1

Situation: A guy at a party is talking to his friend about why he is afraid to walk over and introduce himself to a woman. His friend gives him encouragement.

Idioms: what's eating you?, get something off one's chest, keep something bottled up, (not) have the guts, give it a shot, wouldn't be caught dead with, skip it, bite the bullet, bite someone's head off, bite off more than one can chew, bite your tongue!, put something off, be put off, hit it off, that'll be the day, take the initiative, now you're talking!, be bound to, pass up

Pronunciation point: **sentence stress**

Lesson 2: Smoking—
The Bottom Line   19

Situation: Two people are smoking on an apartment building balcony because they have been asked to smoke outside. They talk about how they dislike the way they are often treated by nonsmokers.

idioms: fed up with, up in arms, look down on, look up to, rub someone the wrong way, rub it in, do without, be taken aback, let it slide, let it go, come to think of it, put out, so as not to, can see one's point, swallow one's pride, in hindsight, the bottom line

Pronunciation point: **stress and linking in two-word verbs**

Review: Crossword Puzzle for Lessons 1 and 2   37

Situation: Two students are sitting at a cafe, talking about two of their professors. One is great, motivating, and inspiring, while the other is a bore.

Idioms: be bored to death, be bored stiff, be bored to tears, stick it out, stick out, spark interest, what a drag, once in a blue moon, an awful lot, someone's mind is wandering, be on the edge of one's seat, it dawned on someone, come down to, boil down to, fool around, bomb a test, buckle down, buckle up, take someone up on something

Pronunciation point: **intonation in statements**

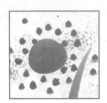

Situation: A reporter is interviewing a homeless man as they sit together on a park bench.

Idioms: in this neck of the woods, live on, live from hand to mouth, dead wrong, dead against, turn (roll) over in one's grave, keep up with, catch up with, pile on, let up, let down, move (climb) up the ladder, get burned out, at stake, day in and day out, close down, blow it, get by, wishful thinking

Pronunciation point: **intonation in questions**

Situation: Michael is at work, and he's telling everyone that he has just won the lottery.

Idioms: what's gotten into __?, not have the slightest idea, have no idea, not have a clue, beats me, your guess is as good as mine, that's unheard of, beyond the shadow of a doubt, to say the least, beyond one's comprehension, sink in, one's heart sank, sink or swim, have a sinking feeling, I've got to hand it to you, let alone, leave alone, in store, be up in the air, make the most of, go down the drain, rule out, be on the lookout, have got it made

Pronunciation point : **thought groups and linking**

Lesson 9: Flying to a Distant Place— A Bad Case of Jet Lag 155

Situation: A young woman has just returned home from a year of study in another country. She is very sleepy because of the time difference, and her father tries to keep her awake by getting her to talk and take a walk.

Idioms: have jet lag, can't keep one's eyes open, be wiped out, stretch out, get a second wind, have one's ups and downs, scratch the surface, in depth, from scratch, hop on/in, it hit home, be wrapped up in, wrap up, be in/get out of one's rut, music to one's ears, be all ears, face the music, to top that off, broach the subject, bring up a subject, sleep on it, mull it over

Pronunciation point: **troublesome consonant sounds**

Lesson 10: Embarrassed— Going Through the Floor 175

Situation: In a restaurant, a woman is telling a friend about problems with her boss. She finds out to her dismay that her boss is in an adjacent booth and hears everything.

Idioms: be in vain, be vain, a good __ minutes, get a word in edgewise, get/be fouled up, foul something up, a foul-up, be under the illusion, be under the impression, go on, come up, get to, you look like you've seen a ghost, go through the floor, blend into the woodwork, I will never live this down, hold/have a grudge against, put one's foot in one's mouth, knock it off, straighten things out, clear the air, could kick oneself, it's over and done with

Pronunciation point: **troublesome vowel sounds**

Review: Crossword Puzzle for Lessons 9 and 10 192

Acknowledgments

Thank you to Heinle & Heinle for giving me this opportunity to create another level of *All Clear*. A very special thank you goes to my wonderful editorial director, Erik Gundersen, who was always supportive, insightful, thorough, and a great pleasure to work with.

To Charles Heinle, President, Stan Galek, Vice President and Publisher, Ken Pratt, associate editor, and John McHugh, national field sales manager, I send my appreciation.

To Margaret Cleveland, my project editor, I knew when you said, "Helen, you're the mother of your book," that we'd work especially well together. And I was right. Thank you for your attention to detail, wonderful feedback, and a job extremely well done. It was a pleasure working with you.

At Heinle & Heinle, I'd also like to thank Kristin Thalheimer, Production Services Coordinator, and Bruno Paul, Market Development & Director for their enthusiastic support and hard work.

To my great friends and colleagues, Sharon Jones, Rosemary Loughman, Rosie Piller, Carmen Rodriguez, and Ellen Rosenfield, I will always be grateful for your absolutely invaluable feedback and support.

And to my daughter, Melissa, thank you for all your patience when I disappeared into the computer world. And thank you, too, for your feedback on the dialogues and expressions. You have a great sense of natural language, and your input is a big part of *All Clear! Advanced.*

To my family, friends, students, and colleagues

Dear Student,

Welcome to *All Clear! Advanced: Idioms and Pronunciation in Context*. As an advanced student of English, you no doubt know how important it is to keep adding to your knowledge of idioms and other expressions.

I've taught students at your level for many years, and have found that the following is what they need and want when studying idioms:

- to recognize and use the most common expressions

- to see numerous examples of the expressions in different contexts and in natural language

- to clarify how these expressions resemble or are different from other expressions they've heard

- to learn how to pronounce these expressions, not only alone, but also as parts of sentences

- to know the grammar associated with each expression

- to know any particular information about the use of expressions—for example, whether an expression is appropriate to say to a boss or a teacher as well as to a best friend

- to have a lot of opportunities to practice using the expressions in both speaking and writing

- to have a good time and do a lot of talking about interesting and meaningful topics in and out of class

If this is what you also want to do, then our goals are the same. To meet these goals, you will work through chapters on various topics that I hope will interest you. Some are controversial, some are about personal and social themes, and some will, hopefully, make you laugh.

Good luck to you, and I hope that you find the material in this text to be *all clear*.

Sincerely,

Helen Kalkstein Fragiadakis

To the Teacher

All Clear! Advanced: Idioms and Pronunciation in Context is an advanced level ESL or EFL text that:

—teaches students to recognize and produce high-frequency American idioms and expressions

—provides numerous contexts containing natural language from which students can infer meanings

—contextualizes the study of pronunciation by integrating it with the study of idioms

—exposes students to conversational situations that can serve as a basis for class discussion with a cross-cultural focus

—provides many structured and communicative activities for listening, speaking, writing, and pronunciation practice

Question:

What makes this idiom text advanced? How is it different from the original *All Clear,* which is intended for intermediate level students?

Answer:

All Clear! Advanced has:

—more expressions per lesson in longer dialogues. The dialogues and exercises contain higher level language.

—a number of somewhat "colorful" expressions that would sound quite strange being used by any but advanced level students.

Question:

How were the expressions in this book chosen?

Answer:

For years, as I heard people use common expressions, I wrote them down on scraps of paper wherever I was. The master list lived on my refrigerator door, but I had notes in the living room, by the bed, in my purse, at work, in the car, etc. The list grew to contain over four hundred expressions, about two hundred of which appear in this text.

General Information

— All Clear Advanced is divided into ten lessons, nine appendices, and five crossword puzzles for review.

— It is possible to move through the text in random order. Each lesson is independent, except in one area: pronunciation. If you plan to make pronunciation a substantial component of your course, you might prefer to follow the lessons in order because the pronunciation points build upon one another.

— Lesson 1 has more detailed instructions than the other lessons. These are intended to help students understand how to deal with the different parts of the lesson. For this reason, you might want to start with Lesson 1.

— You probably won't have the time to cover each exercise in a lesson and will want to pick and choose, especially between Exercises 7, 8, and 9 (Scene Two, Chain Story, Role Playing). These are included to offer a variety of communicative exercises.

— Most activities, from the Warm-Up to the last exercise, can be done in pairs or groups. When students work in groups, you might want to assign roles: leader, reporter, timekeeper, participant. Group leaders should make sure that students know one another's names, that everyone participates in a balanced way, and that the group stays on task and completes the activity at hand.

Lesson Format and Suggestions

Warm-Up:

Students are given a variety of warm-up activities before they deal with the lesson's main dialogue. Warm-up activities include making lists, completing charts and concept (mind) maps, creating new lesson titles, answering questions, agreeing or disagreeing with quotations and making predictions.

Dialogue:

Listed under "Dialogue Steps" are the possible ways to work with the introductory dialogue. Students can read the dialogue as they listen to the tape, say the dialogue in pairs (or in some cases, threes), or perform the dialogue in front of the class.

Guess the Meanings:

Before going into the *Understanding the New Expressions* section, students have the opportunity to guess the meanings of five of the expressions from the dialogue. Paraphrases of the expressions are provided, and students analyze the dialogue to find the expressions that seem to mean the same as the paraphrases. The following are the answers:

Lesson 1: have the guts, give it a shot, (let's just) skip it, That'll be the day, pass up

Lesson 2: get (so) up in arms, so as not to, in hindsight, rubs me the wrong way, the bottom line

Lesson 3: What a drag!, bombed, take you up on, it dawned on me, once in a blue moon

Lesson 4: dead wrong, blew it, at stake, this neck of the woods, let up

Lesson 5: I haven't the slightest idea, that's unheard of, making the most of, you've got it made, What's gotten into?

Lesson 6: lose your head, out of the blue, sit tight, cooped up in, dwell on

Lesson 7: there are no ifs, ands, or buts about it; plugging away at; are a quantum leap over; grapple with; tear me away

Lesson 8: it's nothing to write home about, be held accountable for, a bone of contention, had no bearing on, blowing (this whole thing) out of proportion

Lesson 9: had (my) ups and downs, stretch out, broach the subject, wrapped up in, it hit home

Lesson 10: go on, hold a grudge against me, knock it off, was in vain, straighten things out

Understanding the New Expressions:

In this section, students are given the following:

—brief definitions

—notes on general usage, grammar, pronunciation, and occasionally origin

—additional examples, often in the form of mini-dialogues between Speaker 1 and Speaker 2 (S1 and S2)

—additional expressions that are similar to or in direct contrast to the expressions being studied

Students can work through this section with others and/or on their own. After students read about and perhaps discuss each expression, they indicate whether they understand or still have questions by circling the check mark or question mark that appears next to each expression in the margin. You might encourage your students to highlight any information or examples that are not clear so that when you deal with questions, students know exactly what to ask about.

The following are the directions given to students in this section:

WITH OTHERS:

Work in small groups to go through this information. The leader of each group should make sure that everyone participates equally.

1. Silently read a section about one expression. Then look back at the dialogue to see how that expression is used in conversation.

2. Take turns in your group reading the short dialogues and examples from that section aloud.

3. The leader should ask if there are any questions, and group members should try to give explanations and examples to one another. When necessary, your group can ask members of other groups or your teacher for help.

4. After you discuss each expression, circle the check mark (√) or question mark (?) in the margin to indicate whether or not you understand the information given. If you circle the question mark, then highlight or underline what is still not clear to you.

5. When your class comes back together as a large group, ask questions about what is still not clear.

ON YOUR OWN:

Read this entire section carefully, and for each expression circle the check mark or question mark in the margin to indicate whether or not you understand the information given. If you circle the question mark, then highlight or underline what is still not clear to you. At the next class, your teacher and/or classmates can provide clarification as you ask your questions.

or

List your questions on 3 x 5 cards. Hand in the cards at the next class. Your teacher will hand the cards back out randomly, and students will take turns answering the questions and providing more examples.

Exercises

Exercises move from structured to less and less structured. If you do not have the time to cover all twelve exercises, you will probably want to pick and choose according to the needs and interests of your class.

Exercise 1—Mini-Dialogues: This is a matching exercise that gives students practice in using idioms in very brief conversational exchanges. The best way to check this exercise in class is to have one student read an item from column A aloud and then have another student read the appropriate response from column B so that everyone can hear the mini-dialogues that are created through matching. The answers appear in Appendix E.

When working on pronunciation, you might want to return to this exercise so that students can use these mini-dialogues to practice particular pronunciation points. The mini-dialogues appear on the audio program.

Exercise 2—Choosing the Idiom: This is usually a fill-in-the-blank dialogue or paragraph accompanied by a word list and an illustration. This exercise gives students a chance to see some of the idioms used in another context. Also, when providing answers, students learn to give attention to grammatical factors such as subject-verb agreement and verb tense. The answers appear in Appendix E. This exercise appears on the audio program.

Exercise 3—Dictation: As students listen to the dictation, they write a short paragraph that summarizes the opening dialogue and often contains reported speech. It would be best to use the tape to give the dictation, but if that is not possible, the dictations can be read from Appendix A by the teacher or a student.

It is helpful if the students know the words for punctuation marks: period, comma, question mark, exclamation point, dash, hyphen, colon, semicolon. They should also know what "indent" means.

Dictation Directions

a. While students just listen, read the entire dictation aloud at normal speed, using natural stress and intonation.

b. Give the dictation, pausing at natural points between phrases and sentences while students write.

c. Read the entire dictation once more so that students can check their work.

d. To check students' work:

- collect the dictations, or

- have students exchange papers and circle errors as they look at the corrected dictation on the board, on an overhead transparency, or in Appendix A.

Exercise 4—Pronunciation: Dialogues are frequently used to contextualize the teaching of pronunciation. Here, the numerous dialogues provide examples of and opportunities for practice of many aspects of pronunciation, and while students are working on pronunciation, they are reinforcing their knowledge of the expressions in each lesson.

The following pronunciation points are covered in this text:

- Sentence stress

- Stress and linking in two-word verbs

- Intonation in statements

- Intonation in questions

- Thought groups and linking

- Contractions and reduced forms

- Voiced and voiceless consonants and the –s ending

- Voiced and voiceless consonants and the –ed ending

- Troublesome consonant sounds
- Troublesome vowel sounds

Each lesson focuses on one of the above points, and starting with Lesson 3, each lesson reviews pronunciation points covered in preceding lessons. It is for this reason that you might want to cover lessons in the order presented.

If, perhaps, you would like to cover a pronunciation point that is taught later in the text, you can have the students apply the information from the later lesson to the dialogue in the current lesson.

Answers to some of the pronunciation practice exercises appear in Appendix E, and a number of pronunciation exercises appear on the audio program.

Exercise 5—Questions for Discussion and/or Writing: There are two distinct ways to approach this activity for discussion—students can get into small groups and answer the questions, or they can "mill around" with each other using the *Walk and Talk* activity in Appendix B. The items in Exercise 5 and in Appendix B are identical. The directions for these activities are given with each.

If you would like to give your students more writing practice:

—have them write their own answers to these discussion questions.

—have them look at the notes they took while their classmates answered their questions during the *Walk and Talk* activity and then write more complete sentences. They should include the names of the students who supplied the information, and perhaps *Walk and Talk* again to show their classmates what they wrote so that they can confirm that their sentences are accurate and true.

In both of these writing activities, you may need to remind students to write complete sentences that contain the expressions that appear in the questions.

Exercise 6—Write Your Own: This is a challenging exercise that requires students to write sentences using certain expressions. Students are given specific situations and then asked to write dialogues, monologues, or people's thoughts. Possible "answers" appear in Appendix E. You might want to have your students do this exercise on a separate piece of paper so that you can collect it and possibly even type up some of the student writing.

Corrected student responses to this exercise can also serve as dictations for your students to give each other in pairs or small groups. This would provide a truly communicative situation in which students would have to closely monitor their pronunciation while imparting information containing the new expressions.

Exercise 7—Scene Two: This is basically a dialogue-writing exercise in which students write and then perform a scene that could follow the opening dialogue or the dialogue that appears in Exercise 2. As students work on their own or in pairs or groups, they should be reminded that they do not need to have an idiom in every sentence and, when possible, they should try to incorporate expressions that they learned in preceding lessons. They might refer to the Contents as they write. This is another exercise that could be collected, corrected, and possibly typed up.

Before students perform Scene Two, they should decide on a pronunciation point or two to focus on, and then mark the dialogue accordingly. When they perform the dialogue, they should monitor their pronunciation.

This activity and the Exercise 9 role play are perfect for videotaping. If students are shy about having their videotapes analyzed in class, you can assign them to do a video analysis on their own, outside of class.

When you are working on the first lesson, you may wish to write the dialogue as a class before having students do this exercise on their own or in small groups. Students can suggest lines for the dialogue as you write them on the board, on a transparency, or even on a computer whose image can be projected. Point out the problem if one utterance does not logically follow another so students see immediately that coherence is an important factor in writing dialogues. Discuss grammatical changes that need to be made in the expressions (tense, person, pronouns, etc.).

Exercise 8—Chain Story:
This activity can be done with the entire class or in small groups. The expressions from the lesson should be written on the board or on an overhead transparency. This list can include any expressions from other lessons that you would like to review. To create the list, you can refer to the Contents.

Students sit in a circle. One student starts the chain story by reading the first sentence or sentences supplied in the lesson. The next student creates another sentence to continue the story. To create a coherent story, students will have to listen carefully to one another. For this reason, if a student doesn't understand what has just been said, the previous speaker should repeat his or her sentence, and possibly clarify it.

Students should not feel that each sentence must have an idiom. However, they should be encouraged to look at the idiom list and include expressions when possible. When they speak, they should be monitoring their pronunciation and grammar. If they find themselves absolutely unable to come up with a sentence, they can say "pass."

If you would like to keep the story, you can write what your students say and then give them copies at the next class meeting.

Exercise 9—Role Playing:
This exercise, in contrast to the "Scene Two" exercise, is completely oral.

The following are suggested steps to follow:

a. You or a student write the expressions on the board or on an overhead transparency. It is convenient to refer to the Contents when doing this.

b. Add any other expressions that you would like to review. Be sure that they would somehow fit into the contexts of the suggested role plays.

c. Have the students look at the cartoon and read the explanation of what is going on.

d. Put students into small groups and give them time to briefly (and orally) prepare what they will say. Suggested first lines are provided. Be sure that students understand the context of the role play. If you have a chance to bring in props beforehand, give them out now.

e. Have one group of students come to the front of the class. Remind the group to periodically glance at the board or overhead projector in order to include at least some of the new expressions.

f. As students perform, you can:

- note which idioms were used and plan to comment on how they were pronounced and whether or not they were used correctly in terms of grammar and context.

- videotape the students. The tape can then be replayed for the entire class or privately for only those who performed.

Exercise 10—Tic Tac Toe: Tic Tac Toe requires students to produce grammatically and semantically correct sentences containing the new expressions. This game provides an enjoyable context for review before a quiz. Directions:

a. First play a traditional Tic Tac Toe game so that students become familiar with the strategies involved. Explain that any straight line wins, whether it is horizontal, vertical, or diagonal.

b. Put the Tic Tac Toe grid on the board, and fill in the nine spaces with expressions to be practiced.

c. Divide the class into two teams, X and O. Flip a coin (and teach "heads or tails") to see which team goes first.

d. To get an X or an O in a space, a team has to create a grammatically and semantically correct sentence using the expression that appears there. Allow team members to confer, but enforce a 30-second time limit. Be sure that students take turns giving the answers.

e. The first team to get three X's or O's in a straight line wins.

f. If there are any expressions left uncovered by X's or O's, keep them for another game. Add other expressions to the spaces already used, and play again.

Exercise 11—Expand on What You Now Know: This exercise is essentially a contact assignment that requires students to go out and ask native speakers to explain and provide sample sentences for two-word verbs they haven't yet studied.

The two-word verbs included here contain the same verbs found in two-word verb expressions covered in the lesson, but the particles are different. This activity allows students to expand their knowledge of two-word verbs by essentially clustering them. For example, in Lesson 1 students study *pass up* as in *pass up an opportunity.* Then, in this contact assignment, students find out the meanings of other two-word verbs using the word *pass: pass away, pass back, pass by,* and *pass out.*

Before students do this contact assignment the first time, they should go over the information in Appendix C for information on how to start a conversation with a native speaker.

Exercise 12—Connect Your Class to the Real World: This activity requires students to find three expressions from the "real world" every week. They can keep an inventory in their notebooks or on 3 x 5 cards, following the format in Appendix D. The appendix provides specific directions for creating this collection.

Crossword Review Puzzles

Crossword puzzles require students to supply parts of expressions with the correct spelling. Students unfamiliar with this activity will need "across" and "down" explained. These puzzles follow every two lessons, and their solutions appear in Appendix F.

Student Self-Assessment

To help students become more responsible for their own learning, it is valuable to occasionally ask them to stop and assess how well they are doing and how much effort they are putting in. For this reason, a Student Self-Evaluation Questionnaire is included in Appendix G, and a visual self-evaluation activity called "The Train" is included in Appendix H. Instructions on how to conduct these self-assessments appear in their appendices. You can use these at any time during your course.

Your Assessment of Students

It is well-known that it can be difficult to assign grades in listening/speaking and pronunciation classes because of the nature of the many open-ended activities. The inclusion of idioms in these classes brings in more concrete language material that can easily be assigned as homework and subsequently assessed.

The dictations in Appendix A and the Write Your Own possibilities in the answer key for Exercise 6, in addition to text and student-written dialogues, can be turned into cloze tests. Students can also be given specific situations, possibly accompanied by cartoons or pictures, and then asked to write dialogues using a number of the new expressions.

Cassette Tape

The supplementary cassette tapes use natural speech to present the following from each lesson:

—Opening Dialogue

—Exercise 1—Mini-Dialogues

—Exercise 2—Choosing the Idiom

—Exercise 3—Dictation

—Exercise 4—Pronunciation (certain sections)

I hope you and your students enjoy using this text, and I welcome your comments and suggestions.

Helen Kalkstein Fragiadakis
Contra Costa College
San Pablo, California

At a Party—
Taking the Initiative

Warm-Up

Notice that one of the men in the cartoon is looking at a woman at the party. Write down three words that describe how you think the man feels right now.

_____

_____

_____

Dialogue Steps

Choose one or more of the following:
(a) Listen to the tape as you read the dialogue.
(b) Say the dialogue in pairs.
(c) Have two volunteers perform the dialogue in front of the class.

AL: **What's eating you?**

BILL: What do you mean? I'm fine.

AL: No, you aren't. Come on, whatever it is, **get it off your chest.**

BILL: Well . . . see that woman over there? Her name's Elizabeth. I've been trying to find a way to meet her for months, and now, here she is. But I don't **have the guts** to walk over there.

AL: Come on, Bill, this is your chance. Just **give it a shot.** What do you have to lose?

BILL: She **wouldn't be caught dead with me.**

AL: Why do you say that?

BILL: Oh, let's just **skip it,** OK? I don't know why I even told you.

AL: How do you know her, anyway?

BILL: We work in the same building.

AL: Well, I think you should just **bite the bullet,** go over there, and start a conversation.

BILL: Maybe later.

AL: Why **put it off**? Who knows? You two might **hit it off.**

BILL: **That'll be the day.**

AL: Why are you so negative all of a sudden? I've never seen you like this.

BILL: Maybe you're right. I should just **take the initiative** and walk over there. But what should I say?

AL: **Now you're talking.** Just introduce yourself and start talking about the party or mention that you've seen her at work. She's **bound to** recognize you, too.

BILL: Well, maybe. Oh…you're probably right. If I **pass up** this chance, I'll never forgive myself. Well, here I go. Wish me luck!

Guess the Meanings

When you say the same thing with different words, you are paraphrasing. Below is a list of paraphrases of five of the idiomatic expressions contained in the dialogue. On your own or with a partner, try to guess the five. To do this, make sure that what is written below would easily fit in the dialogue.

Paraphrase	Idiomatic Expression from the Dialogue
Example: What's bothering you?	*What's eating you?*
1. have the courage	_____
2. Try it.	_____
3. (Let's) not talk about it.	_____
4. That will never happen.	_____
5. don't take advantage of	_____

Figure it Out with Others and/or On Your Own

WITH OTHERS:

Work in small groups to go through this information. The leader of each group should make sure that everyone participates equally.

1. Silently read a section about one expression. Then look back at the dialogue to see how that expression is used in conversation.
2. Take turns in your group reading the short dialogues and examples from that section aloud.
3. The leader should ask if there are any questions, and group members should try to give explanations and examples to one another. When necessary, your group can ask members of other groups or your teacher for help.
4. After you discuss each expression, circle the check mark (√) or question mark (?) in the margin to indicate whether or not you understand the information given. If you circle the question mark, then highlight or underline what is still not clear to you.
5. When your class comes back together as a large group, ask questions about what is still not clear.

ON YOUR OWN:

Read this entire section carefully, and for each expression circle the check mark or question mark in the margin to indicate whether or not you understand the information given. If you circle the question mark, then highlight or underline what is still not clear to you. At the next class, your teacher and/or classmates can provide clarification as you ask your questions.

or

List your questions on 3 x 5 cards. Hand in the cards at the next class. Your teacher will hand the cards back out randomly, and students will take turns answering the questions and providing more examples.

All Clear?

√ ?   ## 1. Whát's éating (you)?

Definition: What's bothering you?

S1: I don't want to talk right now.
S2: What's eating you?
S1: Nothing. I'll talk to you later.

S1: What's eating him today? He's in a really bad mood.
S2: I don't know. But let's stay out of his way until he comes out of it.

√ ?   ## 2. gét sómething óff one's chést

Definition: reveal something (usually a confession or complaint) that has been bothering you

S1: I have to **get something off my chest.** It's been bothering me for a long time.
S2: What is it?
   (possible responses)
S1: I don't want you to borrow my car anymore.
   I don't think it's fair that his salary is higher than mine.
   I haven't been honest with you.
   I lied to you.

Contrast the Opposite: **kéep sómething bottled úp (inside)** = keep something that has been bothering you inside.

Negative: **not keep anything bottled up**

S1: It's not healthy to **keep** all those feelings/problems/thoughts **bottled up inside.** You can get sick. You need to talk to someone.
S2: You're right. Can I talk to you?

—I'm **not keeping anything bottled up.** Why are you asking me all these questions?

√ ? **3. (nót) háve the gúts (to)**

Definition: (not) have the courage (to)

—She's a coward. She **doesn't have the guts to** dive off that cliff.
—Do you **have the guts to** swim there? There may be snakes.
—I don't **have the guts to** make a speech in front of the whole class.

√ ? **4. gíve it a shót**

Definition: try something; give something a chance to happen

S1: I was offered a new job.
S2: Will you take it?
S1: Yeah, I think I'll **give it a shot.**

S1: Are you going to go skiing when you go to the mountains?
S2: Yeah, I think I'll **give it a shot.** But if I don't like it, I'll sit by the fireplace and read a good book.

—They're moving across the country. They'll **give it a shot** for six months, and if it doesn't work out, they'll move back.

√ ? **5. (someone) wóuldn't be cáught déad (with someone)**

Definition: (someone) would never want to be with someone because of dislike, fear, or shame

—You know, those two politicians **wouldn't be caught dead with each other.**
—She **wouldn't be caught dead with** those fanatics.
                                        her ex-boyfriend.

Contrast: **wouldn't be caught dead (in a place)**
              wouldn't be caught dead (doing something)

—They **wouldn't be caught dead** in a fast-food restaurant.
—We **wouldn't be caught dead** there.

—I **wouldn't be caught dead riding** in a rocket to the moon.
—He **wouldn't be caught dead reading** those books.

√ ? 6. skíp it

Definition: let's not talk about it anymore

Idiomatic Synonym: **forgét it**

S1: Come on. Tell me what's wrong.
S2: Let's just **skip it**, OK? I don't want to talk about it.

Contrast: **skíp something** = miss something on purpose, not by accident
skíp lines = not write on every line; leave an empty space (line)
skip dessért = not eat dessert
skip óver = intentionally not deal with a certain part of something or certain people:

—When I read the book, I **skipped over** the introduction.
—They **skipped over** us, and picked Marion and Rob to do the job.

√ ? 7. bíte the búllet (and do something)

Definition: make the decision to do something that takes courage ("guts") after hesitating for some time

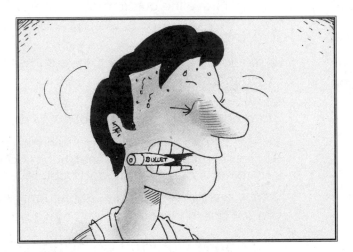

Origin: "This expression comes from the medical profession. During the nineteenth century surgeons were often called on to perform amputations . . . on the battlefield when no anesthesia was available. So the patient would be given a bullet and told to bite hard upon it. The theory was that this . . . would serve to distract somewhat from the attention paid by the patient to the pain of the operation. The basic meaning of the expression *bite the bullet* is that one must act with courage and avoid any show of fear. Rudyard Kipling said it well in his "The Light That Failed": "Bite on the bullet, old man, and don't let them think you're afraid." (Source: *Morris Dictionary of Word and Phrase Origins*)

—Don't keep talking about it. Just **bite the bullet** and do it.
—They **bit the bullet** and got married.
—I'm going to **bite the bullet** and buy that new car.

Contrast other expressions using "bite":

bíte someone's héad off = yell at or criticize someone that you are very angry at

—My mom **bit my head off** when I lost the car keys.

bíte off móre than one can chéw = accept or agree to do more than you can handle, especially work

—When I said I'd do this project, I **bit off more than I could chew,** and now regret it because I have no time for my family or friends.

Bíte your tóngue! = "Don't say that (about the future)! We don't want that to ever happen"!

S1: She has a fever, and I bet tomorrow we'll all be sick.
S2: Bite your tongue!

S1: The next storm/earthquake is going to be worse than this one.
S2: Bite your tongue!

√ ? 8. put something óff

Definition: postpone, delay until later

Grammar Notes: (1) If you use a pronoun in this expression, be sure to put the pronoun *between* the two words. (2) When a verb follows *put off,* it's necessary to add -ing to form a gerund.

S1: You know the expression "Don't **put off** till tomorrow what you can do today"?

S2: Uh-huh.
S1: I do the opposite. I don't do today what I can do tomorrow. How about you?

S1: I'll study later.
S2: Don't **put it off** for too long, or you'll be sorry.

S1: I always **put off** study**ing** until the last minute. I'll never change.
S2: Neither will I.

Contrast: **(be) put óff** = be discouraged or annoyed by someone or something. This expression is in the passive voice, and the two words put and off cannot be separated by other words.

—I was really **put off** by those people. They were very rude.
—I was **put off** by the smell in that restaurant and didn't want to eat there.

√ ? 9. hit it óff

Definition: get along very well immediately (This is said about people who meet for the first time and like each other very much.)

Note: The word *hit* in this expression does not mean that someone actually hits or is hit.

Grammar Note: The basic form of this expression doesn't change. The word *it* is always in the middle. However, the verb tense can change.

—When they met a few months ago, they **hit it off** right away, and now they see each other every day.
—I'm going to meet her parents tomorrow night. I hope we **hit it off.**
—We didn't **hit it off** very well, so I don't think we'll see each other again.

√ ? 10. **That'll be the dáy.**

Definition: That will never happen, in my opinion. Literally, this expression means "I don't expect that day to ever come."

Note: "That'll be the day" is a sarcastic expression because you are saying exactly the opposite of what you mean.

Pronunciation Note: Give the most emphasis to the word *That'll.*

S1: Someday you'll be your own boss and not have to take orders from anyone.
S2: That'll be the day.

S1: They're trying to clean up the pollution here and plant more trees. Eventually our city will look like it did a hundred years ago.
S2: That'll be the dáy.

√ ? 11. **táke the inítiative**

Definition: take the first step in doing something, take action

Pronunciation Note: The *ti* in *initiative* is pronounced like *sh*: /ɪ-nÍ-ʃɪə-tɪv/.

S1: She's very successful, isn't she?
S2: She sure is. That's because she's not afraid to **take the initiative.** She doesn't hesitate to express her ideas and suggest projects. And she doesn't have an ounce of fear in her either.

—Nothing is going to happen if you don't **take the initiative.** You have to take the first step, because no one is going to come to you.
—You can **take the initiative** and:
    start a conversation
    ask someone out (for a date)
    suggest that something be done at work or in school
    write a proposal for a project
    make some phone calls to find something out

√ ? 12. **Nów you're tálking.**

Definition: I didn't agree with what you said or were doing before, but now I completely agree.

Pronunciation Note: Emphasize the word *now.* The point here is that I agree *now,* but I didn't agree before.

S1: Let's take a week's vacation.
S2: Only a week?
S1: OK, a month.
S2: Now you're talking!

S1: You can have the car for $3,000.
S2: Thanks anyway, but I think I'll look around.
S1: How about $2,000?
S2: **Now you're talking!** I'll take it.

√ ? 13. **be bóund to**

Definition: be likely to; be probable

Grammar Note: This expression is usually used in the present tense even though you are talking about the future.

—It's **bound to** rain. Look at the clouds.
—Don't worry about traveling there. Someone **is bound to** speak English.
—Your candidates **are bound to** win. They have a lot of money for advertising.
—She's **bound to** go out with you. After all, you're a great guy.

√ ? 14. **pass úp**

Definition: to miss, not take advantage of an opportunity

Note: Often used as *pass up a chance, pass up an opportunity, pass it up*

Grammar Note: If you use a pronoun in this expression, be sure to put the pronoun *between* the two words.

S1: Can I take two weeks off?
S2: When?
S1: Soon. I won a free trip to Hawaii, and I have to use the ticket within thirty days. I don't want to **pass up** this great opportunity.

—You've got to say something now. It's the perfect time. Don't **pass up** this chance.
—The dessert looks absolutely delicious. But I'm so full that I think I'll have to **pass it up.**

Exercises

1. Mini-Dialogues

Below are three exercises with two columns each, A and B. Column A contains the first lines of dialogues, and column B contains possible responses. For each opening line in column A, choose the *best* response from column B. Sometimes more than one response is possible. Not all responses can be used.

When checking the exercise in class, perform each mini-dialogue. One student should read an item from column A, and another student should respond with the answer from column B.

1. A

____ 1. There they are! It's our chance to get their autographs.
____ 2. What's eating you?
____ 3. Are you going to do it?
____ 4. They're parachute jumping today.
____ 5. Did she ask him out?

1. B

a. I've been keeping something bottled up for a long time.
b. Uh-huh. She bit the bullet and did it.
c. They wouldn't be caught dead there.
d. I know. I could never do that. I don't have the guts.
e. Let's go. I don't want to pass this up.
f. Yup. I'm going to give it a shot.

2. A

____ 1. I think I'm going to skip it. I'm pretty tired.
____ 2. You know, my mistake wasn't the worst thing in the world.
____ 3. Look at how happy they are together.
____ 4. Don't call them. They're busy doing their taxes.
____ 5. We want someone for this job who isn't afraid of taking the initiative.

2. B

a. I know. I'm sorry I bit your head off.
b. Tonight? Wow! They really put them off to the last minute.
c. Let's give it a shot.
d. No problem there. I have a lot of ideas and the guts to try new things.
e. I don't see how you can pass this up.
f. Yeah. I heard they hit it off right away.

3. A

____ 1. I have a confession to make. I bit off more than I can chew, and I need help.
____ 2. I was really put off by the way they acted. They ate in class, and put their feet on the desks.
____ 3. I was going to quit school, but then realized I'd better stay.
____ 4. The weather's never going to get better.
____ 5. Skip over the first three paragraphs, and start with the fourth.

3. B

a. Unbelievable! How rude!
b. Now you're talking.
c. Bite your tongue. It's bound to clear up sooner or later.
d. What page?
e. I have something that I need to get off my chest.
f. I'm not surprised. Let's talk about how to work this out.

2. Choosing the Idiom

You're watching a very emotional TV show with your friend. This is the dialogue that you hear. Fill in the blanks with the best possible expressions from the list. Pay special attention to how the expressions are used grammatically. You may need to consider verb tenses, subject-verb agreement, pronouns, active vs. passive voice, etc. Not all of the expressions in the list can be used. After you finish, practice reading the sentences aloud.

What's eating you
(not) have the guts to
give something a shot
skip it
bite someone's head off
hit it off
take the initiative
be bound to

get off one's chest
keep something bottled up inside
wouldn't be caught dead
skip over
put it off
That'll be the day
bite the bullet
pass up

JULIA: (1) _____? You look absolutely miserable.

JENNIE: Julia, I need some help. I've been offered the leading role in a big

movie, but I (2) _____ say yes.

JULIA: Why not?

JENNIE: Oh, it's one of the actors. We worked on a movie together last year,

and at first, we really (3)_____. But after
a few weeks, I realized she was kind of crazy, and I told myself that I

(4) _____ working with her ever again.

JULIA: And now you don't want to (5)_____this
chance to be a star?

JENNIE: You got it. What am I going to do? The movie (6) _____

_____ be a big success. It's a great story, and the director
is excellent.

JULIA: Why don't you talk to him? Tell him that you have something to

(7) _____.

JENNIE: Yeah, right. I'm going to tell him that I won't work with his wife.

JULIA: His wife? This is getting really complicated.

JENNIE: I know I should (8) _____ and say

something to him. And I can't (9) _____
any longer because he needs to know my decision. But what am I
going to say? "Steven, I have to tell you that I want the part in the
movie, but I can't work with your wife."

JULIA: Are you going to explain why?

JENNIE: How can I complain to him about his wife? He'll (10) _____

_____.

JULIA: Maybe not. (11)_____, and maybe he'll
understand.

JENNIE: (12) _____!

3. Dictation

Your teacher or one of your classmates will read the dictation for this lesson from Appendix A, or you will listen to the dictation on the audio program. You will hear the dictation three times. First, just listen. Second, as you listen, write the dictation on a separate piece of paper. Third, check what you have written.

4. Pronunciation—Sentence Stress

This exercise will help you learn which words are usually, but not always, stressed (emphasized) in a phrase or sentence. Stressed words are the most important words in phrases and sentences because they carry the most information. Native speakers of English stress words that are the most important by making them stronger than the other words. They do this by making the stressed syllables in these words longer.

Practice 1

To find out which words (nouns, verbs, prepositions, and other parts of speech) are usually stressed, look at the *Understanding the New Expressions* section and notice which words have stress marks. Then, on your own or with a partner, complete this chart by putting a check in the appropriate column.

Skip numbers 2 *(bottled up)*, 6 *(skip over)*, 8 *(put something off)*, 9 *(hit it off)*, and 14 *(pass up)* because these are "two-word verbs" that follow a special rule that will be explained in Lesson 2.

	Usually Stressed	Usually Unstressed
Nouns	√	
Pronouns		
Main Verbs		
Verb *be*		
Affirmative Helping Verbs		
Negative Helping Verbs		
Adjectives		
Adverbs		
Conjunctions		
Prepositions		
Articles		
This/that/these/those		
Wh question words		

Note: The answers for this exercise can be found in the Answer Key in Appendix E.

Practice 2

After you have completed the chart, go back to the *Understanding the New Expressions* section and say each expression aloud. Emphasize the stressed words.

Practice 3: Listen and Speak

Focus on listening for the stressed words in the taped Mini-Dialogues in Exercise 1. Listen to one mini-dialogue, and underline or circle the stressed words. Then say that mini-dialogue with a partner. Continue this procedure throughout the exercise.

Example:

A: <u>There</u> they <u>are!</u>* It's our <u>chance</u> to <u>get</u> their <u>autographs.</u>

B: <u>Let's</u> <u>go.</u> I <u>don't</u> <u>want</u> to <u>pass</u> <u>this</u> <u>up.</u>

Practice 4:Listen and Speak

Listen again to the recording of all or part of the first dialogue sentence by sentence to see if the words you expect to be stressed are indeed stressed. As you listen, underline or circle the stressed words. Then perform the dialogue with a partner, giving special attention to sentence stress.

5. Questions for Discussion and/or Writing

Two ways you can ask and answer these questions *orally:*

- You can sit in groups of three or four, with one person being the discussion leader. This person should make sure that you all know one another's names and that everyone participates. At the end of this activity, your teacher may ask the leader or another member of the group to tell the class about the most interesting parts of the conversation.

- You can all *Walk and Talk.* This means that you get out of your seats and ask different students questions containing the new expressions. As you speak to each partner, take short notes on the *Walk and Talk* form for this lesson in Appendix B.

*Pronunciation Note: When forms of "be" come at the end of a sentence, they are stressed.

When you are talking to classmates, be sure to look into their eyes, nod your head, and smile once in a while. If you write, don't write too much because this is a speaking activity, and don't look down at your book too often. And, when possible, try to use the new expressions in your conversation.

If you have a limited amount of time, read the questions ahead of time and mark those that are the most interesting to you. You can then devote your time to discussing only those questions.

Two ways you can answer these questions *in writing:*

● Write your own answers to the questions. Be sure to write complete sentences that contain the expressions in the questions.

● If you have done the *Walk and Talk* activity, write the responses of the students you talked to. Give their names and include the expressions that appeared in the questions. To be sure that your sentences contain the correct information, you can *Walk and Talk* again to show your writing to the students who supplied the information.

Questions

1. Are you the kind of person who keeps things that bother you bottled up inside, or do you get things off your chest? Explain, and give some examples.
2. What are two activities or sports that scare you? Why don't you have the guts to do those things?
3. What is something that you wouldn't be caught dead doing? Who is someone that you wouldn't want to be caught dead with? Name a place where you wouldn't be caught dead. Give your reasons.
4. Have you ever bitten off more than you could chew? Describe what happened.
5. Do you generally do things on time, or do you put things off? Explain by giving some examples.
6. What are some things that people do that put you off?
7. Have you ever hit it off with anyone immediately? Explain the circumstances.
8. What is life bound to be like in the 21st century?
9. What is one kind of food that you can never pass up?
10. What are two ways students can take the initiative to speak to native speakers of English?

6. Write Your Own

Here are some situations along with expressions from this lesson. Use your imagination and write your own sentences or dialogues to describe, explain, or act out the situations.

Example: You have just met your boyfriend's or girlfriend's parents. These are your thoughts. *(put off, hit it off)*

I can't believe that I **put off** meeting them for weeks. It was much better than I expected. We really **hit it off**. I don't know why I was so sure they wouldn't like me.

Try to use at least two of the expressions in parentheses.

1. You are trying to encourage a child you know to tell you what's wrong. He came home from school looking very unhappy. Write what you say to the child. *(What's eating you, keep something bottled up, be bound to)*

    _____

    _____

    _____

    _____

    _____

2. You are encouraging a friend to not pass up a great opportunity to take a new job or attend a university in a different city. Your friend is nervous about leaving and starting something new. Write what you say to your friend. *(pass up, give something a shot, be bound to, have the guts)*

    _____

    _____

    _____

    _____

    _____

3. A husband and wife on a TV show are having an argument. One believes that the other works too much in a new job and doesn't have enough time for the family. Write the conversation between the husband and wife. *(get something off one's chest, bite off more than one can chew, That'll be the day)*

A: _____

B: _____

_____

_____

_____

Choose one of your corrected "Write Your Own" sections and dictate it to a partner or group or your entire class. Before you do this, think about the rules for sentence stress and mark the stressed words.

7. Scene Two

Consider the opening dialogue between the two men to be the first scene of a play. On your own, with a partner, or in a small group, write Scene Two (in other words, write a dialogue). What does Bill say when he finally walks over to Elizabeth? Continue the conversation, with Bill and Elizabeth getting to know each other.

As you write, see if any of the expressions from this lesson fit into the conversation. Also, feel free to use other expressions that you know. But don't feel that it is necessary to have an idiom in every sentence.

If possible, groups of students can practice various versions of Scene Two and then perform them for the class. You might even want to videotape these scenes.

8. Chain Story

Here is the beginning of a story. Continue the story by going around the room and having each student orally add a sentence, or get into small groups and have group members each add a sentence one by one. Try to have three to five expressions in your story. It will be helpful if the expressions are written on the board for all to see.

Some relatives gave me a computer for my birthday. Well, I pretended to be happy, but I was really terrified. I knew I would never learn how to use it, and I also knew that some day they were going to ask me how I was doing with it. I was really worried, but I didn't even take the computer out of the box for a very long time. Then, one day . . . .

9. Role Playing

Using the new expressions from this lesson, act out the following role play. The new expressions should be written on the board.

A young couple is at a fancy restaurant, and they see a very elegant and famous couple at another table. The young couple is talking about whether or not and how to approach the famous people for autographs.

Possible starting lines: *I can't stand it. We have to meet them. What are we going to do?*

10. Tic Tac Toe

In this variation of tic tac toe, to get an X or an O you need to create a grammatically correct sentence that is logical in meaning. Here is a game to start you off. Create as many games as you like, using expressions from Lesson 1.

11. Expand on What You Now Know

In this lesson, you studied expressions with certain verbs. Many more expressions exist in combination with these words.

You already know:

pass up   **put** off

To learn some more expressions with these words, with a partner ask a native speaker to help you fill out this chart. In order to do this kind of assignment, see Appendix C, "Contact Assignments," for information on how to start a conversation with a native speaker of English.

	Meaning	**Sample Sentence**
pass		
away	_____	_____
		_____
back	_____	_____
		_____
by	_____	_____
		_____
out	_____	_____
		_____
put		
in for	_____	_____
	_____	_____

12. Connect Your Class to the Real World

Every week, on your own or with a partner, find three expressions from the real world that are new to you. Keep an inventory in your notebook or on 3 x 5 cards, following the format in Appendix D, "Student Idiom Collection." Be ready to share what you found in small groups or with your entire class.

Smoking—
The Bottom Line

Warm-Up

● Why do you think the woman in this cartoon is so angry?

● On the left, give two or three arguments for smokers' rights, and on the right give two or three arguments for the rights of nonsmokers.

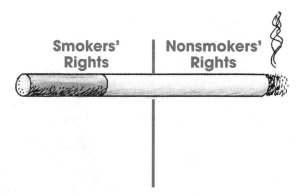

Dialogue Steps

Choose one or more of the following:

(a) Listen to the tape as you read the dialogue.
(b) Say the dialogue in pairs.
(c) Have two volunteers perform the dialogue in front of the class.

WOMAN: Aren't you **fed up with** being sent outside to smoke? I really miss the good old days. Now people **get** so **up in arms** when I smoke, they make me feel like a criminal.

MAN: I know what you mean.

WOMAN: And what I really don't like is the way people **look down on** us. It really **rubs me the wrong way.**

MAN: How do you know they look down on you?

WOMAN: I know they do. OK—here's an example. Last week at work—it was a rainy day—I was waiting for the elevator and holding a pack of cigarettes. I was going to go outside to smoke, and I wasn't bothering anybody. This guy looks at me and says, "Can't you **do without** those things? Are you so addicted that you have to go outside in the pouring rain to smoke?" Well, I **was** so **taken aback!** I couldn't believe that anyone could talk to me like that. But I just looked away and **let it slide.**

MAN: **Come to think of it**, something like that happened to me at a party just like this one. I was sitting outside smoking, not bothering anybody, and a couple came out and asked me to **put out** my cigarette. I told them that I'd come outside to smoke **so as not to** bother anyone inside, and that I wanted to finish my cigarette. Actually, I was very polite. But the woman said it was unfair of me to make others breathe my second-hand smoke outside as well as inside. I **could see her point,** but at the same time, I felt that I had the right to smoke somewhere.

WOMAN: So what did you do?

MAN: **I swallowed my pride** and put my cigarette out. Now, **in hindsight,** I'm not sure it was the right thing to do.

WOMAN: I wouldn't have put it out. **The bottom line,** you know, is that we have rights, too.

Guess the Meanings

Below is a list of paraphrases of five of the idiomatic expressions contained in the dialogue. On your own or with a partner, try to guess the five.

Paraphrase	Idiomatic Expression from the Dialogue
1. get angry	_____
2. in order not to	_____
3. looking back	_____
4. annoys me	_____
5. the main point	_____

■ Understanding the New Expressions

Figure It Out with Others and/or On Your Own

WITH OTHERS:

Work in small groups to go through this information. The leader of each group should make sure that everyone participates equally.

1. Silently read a section about one expression. Then look back at the dialogue to see how that expression is used in conversation.
2. Take turns in your group reading aloud the short dialogues and examples from that section.
3. The leader should ask if there are any questions, and group members should try to give explanations and examples to one another. When necessary, your group can ask members of other groups or your teacher for help.
4. After you discuss each expression, circle the check mark (√) or question mark (?) in the margin to indicate whether or not you understand the information given. If you circle the question mark, then highlight or underline what is still not clear to you.
5. When your class comes back together as a large group, ask questions about what is still not clear.

ON YOUR OWN:

Read this entire section carefully, and for each expression circle the check mark or question mark in the margin to indicate whether or not you understand the information given. If you circle the question mark then highlight or underline what is still not clear to you. At the next class, your teacher and/or classmates can provide clarification as you ask your questions.

or

List your questions on 3 x 5 cards. Hand in the cards at the next class. Your teacher will hand the cards back randomly, and students will take turns answering the questions and providing more examples.

All Clear?

√ ?

1. be fed úp (with something or someone)

Definition: be tired of and disgusted with something or someone

Grammar Note: When *with* is used, this expression is followed by a noun or gerund.

S1: You got a new car?
S2: Uh-huh. I **was fed up with** the old car breaking down every two weeks, and I **was fed up with** my husband's complaints about it.

S1: You**'re fed up with** eat**ing** turkey all week, I can tell.
S2: It's true . . . we've been eating turkey for five days now.

S1: I **am** so **fed up**! Every time we try to start a conversation, the phone rings.
S2: We don't have to answer it.

√ ? 2. gét (be) úp in árms (when/about)

Definition: become very angry

Note: Think of people waving their arms in anger or think of people armed with weapons and ready for battle.

S1: Why do you **get** so **up in arms when** we talk about politics? Why can't we have a calm conversation?

S2: Because we never agree, and I can't understand where you get most of your views. You just won't listen to reason.

S1: Don't talk to her about politics or smoking or abortion . . . anything controversial.

S2: Why?

S1: Because she **gets** all emotional and **up in arms about** the subject, and it's impossible to reason with her.

S1: Don't go near the boss today.

S2: What's the problem?

S1: He's **up in arms about** last month's losses.

√ ? 3. look dówn on (someone or something)

Definition: feel or act as if someone or something is inferior

Grammar Note: The parts of this verb cannot be separated. This verb is used in both active and passive voice.

S1: I hate the way waiters in expensive restaurants **look down on** customers. They act like the customers don't know anything about good food.

S2: And I hate the way some customers **look down on** waiters and waitresses and treat them like servants.

—Isn't it terrible the way older kids at school often **look down on** the younger kids?

—Some language dialects **are looked down on** because they are not the standard used by the majority of people. That's too bad, because dialects represent the cultures of people who speak them.

Contrast the Opposite: **look úp to (someone)** = feel/show respect for someone

S1: He really **looks up to** his big sister, doesn't he? He copies everything she does.

S2: That's for sure. And she loves it.

S1: No one **looks up to** him anymore. That's why they don't think he'll be re-elected.

S2: I don't know about that. He still gets a lot of respect in some communities.

Note: Don't confuse "look up to" with the more literal expression, "look up at." When you "look up to" someone, you feel respect. When you "look up at" someone or something, you are literally tilting your neck to see something that is higher than you. You would "look up *at*" the sky.

√ ?   4. rúb someone the wróng wáy

Definition: annoy or irritate

S1: What do you think of the new guy in the office?

S2: He seems pretty nice. Why do you ask?

S1: I don't know. But there's something about him that **rubs me the wrong way.** Maybe it's because he's always smiling so much. It doesn't seem real.

S1: Did you hear what she just said?

S2: Uh-huh. What's wrong?

S1: Well, it **rubbed me the wrong way.**

Contrast another expression with "rub":   **rub it ín** = emphasize something the listener isn't happy about so that the listener feels bad.

S1: You know that he got two great job offers in one week?

S2: **Don't rub it in!** You know that I'm still job-hunting.

S1: If you hadn't lost the whole file on the computer, we wouldn't be in this situation.

S2: Why do you keep **rubbing it in?** I feel bad enough already.

√ ?   **5. do withóut (something)**

Definition: live without; manage without something

S1: Do you think you could **do without** money and cars and TV and . . . .
S2: I can easily **do without** TV, but money? I don't know.

√ ?   **6. be táken abáck (by a comment or some news)**

Definition: be very surprised because something negative happened that you didn't expect

Origin: *Aback* is a sailing term that is used when movement of a boat is suddenly stopped because the sails press against the mast. When this happens, people on the boat are surprised.

Note: This expression has negative connotations and always occurs in the passive voice.

S1: Instead of thanking me for all my hard work, she actually said nothing. She just took the report. I **was** really **taken aback**. Then later she apologized for not thanking me. She said she'd had something on her mind and wasn't thinking straight.
S2: What did you say?
S1: I told her not to worry about it. And I really appreciated the fact that she admitted that she had been rude and apologized.

—I **was taken aback** *by* what they said.
—I **was taken aback** *when* I heard what they said.

√ ?   **7. lét it slíde**

Definition: not deal with a comment or an issue; just let it pass without saying anything or taking any action

Idiomatic Synonym: **lét it gó**

Grammar Note: The *it* in this expression doesn't change. The expression is always used exactly as it is. (The past of *let* is *let*.)

S1: Did you hear what they said about my team? That's a big lie, and I want them to know how I feel.

S2: Calm down. Just **let it slide**. Leave it alone. You don't want to say anything now that you'll regret later.

√ ? 8. cóme to thínk of it, . . .

Definition: I just thought of something related to our conversation.

Note: This is a transitional expression often used in conversation. Its form does not change.

S1: I need to find someone who wants to have a conversation exchange with me. Do you know anyone who might be interested?

S2: Hmm. **Come to think of it**, I do know someone. But I don't have his number on me. Why don't you give me a call later, and I'll give it to you?

S1: How about dinner Saturday night?

S2: Sounds great. What do you have in mind?

S1: Chinese?

S2: My favorite. Which one?

S1: The one on University Avenue is good. **Come to think of it**, though, it just went out of business. Why don't we try the one on College Avenue?

√ ? 9. put something óut

Definition: extinguish a flame, as in put out a cigarette or put out a fire

Grammar Note: If a pronoun is used, it must go in the middle of the expression.

The teenagers { **put out** their cigarettes / **put** their cigarettes **out** / **put** them **out** } just before their parents came home.

Contrast other meanings of "put out":

—**Put out** (extend) your hand. I have a surprise for you.
—There are people at the door. Can you **put** the dog **out** (put it outside) so he won't bother them?
—They're **putting out** (producing; coming out with) a new computer next month. I can't wait to see it.

S1: Can I give you a lift (ride) home?

S2: Thank you. That's so nice. But I don't want to **put** you **out** (bother you).

S1: Really, it's no bother at all. It's on my way.

—She **was** really **put out** (was bothered) when they canceled dinner at the last minute (note passive voice).

√ ? 10. so as nót to

Definition: in order to avoid doing something undesirable

Grammar Note: The sentence pattern for this expression is: ____ (do something) **so as not to** ____ (cause a negative reaction).

—He was driving very carefully on the ice **so as not to** skid (in order to avoid skidding).

—She didn't tell them the truth **so as not to** hurt their feelings (in order to avoid hurting their feelings).

—The President called a special press conference **so as not to** appear as if he had anything to hide (in order to avoid appearing like he had something to hide).

√ ? 11. **(can) sée someone's póint**

Definition: admit that someone has made a valid point

S1: We should try to watch some TV in English just for a while every day. That way we'll hear the pronunciation, more idioms . . .
S2: I **can see your point,** but it's so hard to understand!

S1: I told her we'd save a lot of money if we drive.
S2: She told me she **sees your point,** but she wants to fly anyway. You two need to talk to each other about what to do.

√ ? 12. **swállow one's príde** (and do something)

Definition: do something even though it makes one feel humiliated (not at all proud)

S1: She left him for another guy, and then she invited him to the wedding!
S2: You're kidding! What did he do?
S1: He **swallowed his pride** and went. And he even bought them a nice gift!

S1: You know you haven't gotten a raise in five years. Don't you think it's time to **swallow your pride** and go see your boss?
S2: You're right. I should have done that years ago.

√ ? **13. in híndsight**

> *Definition:* Now, looking back at the past, a person sees that what she or he did was right or wrong.
>
> *Grammar Note:* Use this form: In hindsight, (subject + verb) . . . It is common to say: "In hindsight, we should have . . . "
>
> **S1:** Their son changed to a new school last year. **In hindsight,** that was a mistake.
> **S2:** Why do you say that?
> **S1:** He's made some friends who aren't interested in school. He doesn't seem to be taking school seriously anymore.
>
> **S1:** I don't mind being a nurse, but now, **in hindsight,** I see that I should have become a doctor.
> **S2:** It's never too late. You can go back to school.

√ ? **14. the bóttom líne (is that . . .)**

> *Definition:* the basic truth, the main point
>
> *Origin:* This expression originally related to profits and losses in business.
>
> **S1:** I know you want to show me the details about the budget. But first, I want to know the **bottom line.** How much did we lose last year?
> **S2:** Twenty million.
>
> **S1:** I know you're a vegetarian. I know you eat only organic foods. I know you get enough sleep. I know you exercise daily. But **the bottom line** is that you've got to quit smoking.
> **S2:** I can see your point.

Exercises

1. Mini-Dialogues

Below are two exercises with two columns each, A and B. Column A contains the first lines of dialogues, and column B contains possible responses. For each opening line in column A, choose the *best* response from column B. Sometimes more than one response is possible. Not all responses can be used.

When checking the exercise in class, perform each mini-dialogue. One student should read an item from column A, and another student should respond with the answer from column B.

1. A

____ 1. You said you'd be here at 7. It's 8:30! When are you ever . . . ?

____ 2. It was my fault, I know, but it's so hard for me to apologize.

____ 3. I could borrow from my parents so that we can go . . .

____ 4. Listen, I can teach you how to use that. Why don't I come over later?

____ 5. It's over. She doesn't return your calls. Why do you think she still wants to see you?

____ 6. Why didn't you invite her to dinner too?

____ 7. The TV's broken. Help!

1. B

a. Listen, the bottom line is that we just don't have the money.

b. Can't you do without it? Are you addicted?

c. Don't get up in arms. I made a mistake, and I'm sorry.

d. That's really nice, but I don't want to put you out.

e. Come to think of it, I know where you can get one.

f. I guess I can see your point.

g. Why don't you just swallow your pride and do it?

h. I thought she rubbed you the wrong way.

2. A

____ 1. In the past, people respected their political leaders.

____ 2. There he goes again . . . insulting my political views.

____ 3. Why didn't she turn on the lights?

____ 4. Do you know where there's an ATM around here?

____ 5. We should have gone somewhere else for vacation.

____ 6. Did they ask you a lot of personal questions too?

____ 7. Why did he quit?

____ 8. You needed only one more number to win the lottery.

2. B

a. Hmm. Come to think of it, there's one right around the corner.

b. I know. There's no one to really look up to anymore.

c. They sure did, and we were really taken aback.

d. Please don't rub it in. It hurts.

e. That may be true in hindsight, but we're here now, so let's try to enjoy it.

f. Just ignore him. Let it slide.

g. So as not to bother anyone, she was trying to be considerate.

h. It's not right to look down on people.

i. He was fed up with office politics.

2. Choosing the Idiom

A guy is reading a book that contains the thoughts of smokers and nonsmokers about smoking. Right now he is reading about an experience of a nonsmoker. Fill in the blanks with the best possible expressions from the list. Pay special attention to how the expressions are used grammatically. You may need to consider verb tenses, subject-verb agreement, pronouns, active vs. passive voice, etc. Not all of the expressions in the list can be used. After you finish, practice reading the sentences aloud.

the bottom line	rub someone the wrong way
can see someone's point	get up in arms
swallow one's pride	fed up with
in hindsight	let it slide
taken aback	do without
so as not to	look down on

I was at a party last week. You know how I (1) _____

_____ when people around me smoke. I always sneeze, and anyway,
I'm afraid of second-hand smoke.

Well, these people started to light up (smoke) in the living room, and I
was so (2) _____that I got up and asked them to
go outside. You should have seen how they looked at me! One of them said

that she was (3) _____always being sent outside

to smoke. I didn't want to get into an argument, so I (4) _____

_____ and didn't say anything. But the guy spoke up and said that
it was time for people to be more polite to smokers. He said that he was tired

of being (5) _____, that nonsmokers have this
superior attitude.

I (6) _____ and said I was sorry if I had
sounded rude because I didn't mean to be. I told them that I was allergic to
smoke, and knew that other people in the room didn't like the smoke either.

I just wanted them to go outside (7) _____
bother anyone. Well, they just turned around and went outside. I have to admit

that I didn't like their attitude. They really (8) _____ .

When will smokers ever realize that they aren't welcome anymore

because they pollute our air? (9) _____
is good health, isn't it?

3. Dictation

Your teacher or one of your classmates will read the dictation for this lesson
from Appendix A, or you will listen to the dictation on the audio program.
You will hear the dictation three times. First, just listen. Second, as you listen,
write the dictation on a separate piece of paper. Third, check what you
have written.

4. Pronunciation Part 1: Stress in Two-Word Verbs

"Two-word verbs" are expressions with idiomatic meanings. These expressions are composed of verbs + words such as *in, on, at, up, down, out,* and *about.* Many of these small words are prepositions.

In this exercise you will learn to stress (emphasize) the second part of two-word verbs. You learned in Lesson 1 that we don't usually stress prepositions. In two-word verbs, however, we make an exception—we stress the preposition more than the main verb.

Grammar Points to Remember About Two-Word Verbs:

● When these expressions actually have three words (such as *fed up with* and *look down on*), you cannot add words inside the expressions. They cannot be separated. They are "inseparable."

● When these expressions are in the passive voice (such as *be put off* by something), they cannot be separated.

● When two-word verbs can be separated, they are called "separable." You can put words between them. For example,

He bottled up his feelings.	Please put out your cigarette.
He bottled *his feelings* up.	Please put *your cigarette* out.
He bottled *them* up.	Please put *it* out.

Incorrect: He bottled up them.   Please put out it.

Notice that when a pronoun is used, it must come in the middle of the expression. It cannot come at the end.

Practice 1

Say these two-word verbs from Lessons 1 and 2 aloud. Make the capitalized words stronger and louder than the other words.

From Lesson 1	**From Lesson 2**
bottled UP	fed UP with
put something OFF	look DOWN on
hit it OFF	look UP to
pass UP	rub it IN
	do WITHOUT
	put OUT

Practice 2

With a partner, practice saying the following sentences. All are about learning English idioms:

1. I can't keep this *bottled UP* anymore. I'm tired of studying so hard!
2. I've always wanted to learn a lot of idioms, but I *put it OFF* for a long time because I was so busy studying grammar.
3. When I first heard the expression *hit it OFF,* I thought two people were hitting each other!
4. Now I have an opportunity to learn idioms. I don't want to *pass it UP.*
5. Sometimes I'm *fed UP with* all this hard work, but I'll keep trying.

6. *Look DOWN on* must be a three-word verb.
7. *Look UP to* also has three words. I guess we should always stress the second word.
8. I know you know all these expressions well. Don't *rub it IN.* I'm trying.
9. My dictionary is something I can't *do WITHOUT.* But I've found that a lot of idioms aren't even in my dictionary.
10. Do you have any idea how many meanings the expression *put OUT* has?

Pronunciation Part 2: Linking in Two-Word Verbs

To "link" means to connect. In English we often link words when one word ends in a consonant sound and the next word starts with a vowel sound. The same happens when a word ends in a vowel sound and the next word starts with a consonant sound. This often occurs in two-word verbs. (For more information on and practice with linking, see Lesson 5.)

Here are examples from Lesson 1:

Expression	**Sounds like**	
bottled ‿ up	boddle-DUP*	/bɑdl-dʌ́p/
put ‿ it ‿ off	pu-di-DOFF*	/pə-dɪ-dɔ́f/
hit ‿ it ‿ off	hi-di-DOFF*	/hɪ-dɪ-dɔ́f/
pass ‿ up	pa-SUP	/pæ-sʌ́p/

Practice 3

● Go back to Practice 2 and insert linking lines between the words that should be linked in the two-word verbs. For example, number 1 would be like this: bottled ‿ up.

● Practice saying these two-word verb expressions aloud.

● Since the same pronunciation rule about linking vowel and consonant sounds applies to spoken English in general, you can also draw linking lines elsewhere in these sentences—for example, "I've‿always wanted to‿learn‿a‿lot‿of‿idioms." After you draw the lines, say the sentences aloud.

Practice 4: Put It All Together

● Locate the two-word verbs in the dialogues from Lessons 1 and 2. Circle the parts of two-word verbs that should be stressed. Draw linking lines between the words that should be connected when spoken.

● Concentrate on stress and linking as you recite one of the dialogues with a partner.

---

*Notice that the *t*'s in these words sound like *d*'s. This situation occurs when:

•the *t* comes between vowel sounds as in *letter, what are,* etc.

•the *t* comes between a vowel and *l* as in *bottle*

Practice 5: Listen and Speak

Listen again to the dialogues in Lessons 1 and 2. Pay special attention to the pronunciation of two-word verbs. If you can, record yourself and compare your pronunciation of two-word verbs to the pronunciation on the tape.

5. Questions for Discussion and/or Writing

Two ways you can ask and answer these questions *orally:*

● You can sit in groups of three or four, with one person being the discussion leader. This person should make sure that you all know one another's names and that everyone participates. At the end of this activity, your teacher may ask the leader or another member of the group to tell the class about the most interesting parts of the conversation.

● You can all *Walk and Talk.* This means that you get out of your seats and ask different students questions containing the new expressions. As you speak to each partner, take short notes on the *Walk and Talk* form for this lesson in Appendix B.

If you have a limited amount of time, read the questions ahead of time and mark those that are the most interesting to you. You can then devote your time to discussing only those questions.

Two ways you can answer these questions *in writing:*

● Write your own answers to the questions. Be sure to write complete sentences that contain the expressions in the questions.

● If you have done the *Walk and Talk* activity, write the responses of the students you talked to. Give their names and include the expressions that appeared in the questions. To be sure that your sentences contain the correct information, you can *Walk and Talk* again to show your writing to the students who supplied the information.

Questions

1. Is there anyone in your family that you don't particularly like? If yes, what is it about his or her personality that rubs you the wrong way?
2. Who did you look up to as a child, and why?
3. In your native culture, what types of behavior are looked down on?
4. Think about something you did in the past (getting married, moving to a certain place, picking this place to study English, voting for a particular candidate in an election). Now, in hindsight, did you make the right decision? Explain.
5. List three things that you can do without and three things that you can't do without.
6. Can you think of a situation in which someone said something critical about you or asked you a personal question and you were very taken aback? What did you do?
7. Is there anything that you are fed up with right now? Explain.

6. Write Your Own

Here are some situations along with expressions from this lesson. Use your imagination and write your own sentences or dialogues to describe, explain, or act out the situations. Try to use at least two of the expressions in parentheses.

1. One of your classmates has asked to borrow some money. You are very surprised and afraid that you won't get the money back, but you lend the money because you want to avoid hurting the person's feelings. The next day, your classmate pays you back. Write about what happened. *(taken aback, so as not to, in hindsight)* (Also be sure to include these phrases: borrow *from*, lend *to*, pay back.)

_____

_____

_____

_____

_____

2. You are driving in rush-hour traffic. You make a momentous decision (a decision that will change your life forever): you will quit your job and move to a smaller city. When you get home, you explain your decision to your family. Write what you say. *(fed up with, do without, the bottom line)*

_____

_____

_____

_____

_____

3. A friend of yours keeps making negative comments about your new girlfriend/boyfriend. Yesterday you didn't say anything, but today you are angry and say so. Write what you say to your friend. *(swallow pride, let it slide, rub the wrong way)*

_____

_____

_____

_____

_____

Choose one of your corrected "Write Your Own" sections and dictate it to a partner or group or your entire class. Before you do this, think about the rules for sentence stress and stress in two-word verbs, and mark the stressed words.

7. Scene Two

Consider the opening dialogue between the man and woman to be the first scene of a play. On your own, with a partner, or in a small group, write Scene Two (in other words, write a dialogue). What happens after they finish their cigarettes? Do they go back into the party? Do other people from the party come outside to the balcony to join them? Do smokers confront nonsmokers?

As you write, see if any of the expressions from this or other lessons fit into the conversation. Also, feel free to use other expressions that you know. But don't feel that it is necessary to have an idiom in every sentence.

If possible, groups of students can practice various versions of Scene Two and then perform them for the class. You might even want to videotape these scenes.

8. Chain Story

Here is the beginning of a story. Continue the story by going around the room and having each student orally add a sentence, or get into small groups and have group members each add a sentence one by one. Try to have three to five expressions in your story. It will be helpful if the expressions are written on the board for all to see.

I have to tell you what happened to me last summer at the airport. I was just starting my vacation, and I showed my ticket and passport to the ticket agent. She typed something on her computer, and then asked me to wait while she checked on something. Then, before I knew what was happening, four airport police officers surrounded me . . .

9. Role Playing

Using the new expressions from this lesson, act out the following role play. The new expressions should be written on the board.

Two people are at a club or disco, and the place is very smoky. One person doesn't mind the smoke, but the other doesn't like it and wants to leave. They argue.

Possible starting line: *I'm really fed up with this smoke. Let's leave.*

10. Tic Tac Toe

In this variation of tic tac toe, to get an X or an O you need to create a grammatically correct sentence that is logical in meaning. Here is a game to start you off. Create as many games as you like, using expressions from Lesson 2. And if you would like to review expressions from Lesson 1, add them to the game.

11. Expand on What You Now Know

In this lesson, you studied two-word verbs with the words *look* and *put*. Many more expressions exist in combination with these verbs.

You already know:

look down on   **put** out
    up to
    up at

To learn some more expressions with these words, with a partner ask a native speaker to help you fill out this chart. In order to do this kind of assignment, see Appendix C, "Contact Assignments," for information on how to start a conversation with a native speaker of English.

Pronunciation Note: Remember to stress the second part of two-word verbs.

	Meaning	Sample Sentence
look		
after	_____	_____
		_____
like	_____	_____
		_____
into	_____	_____
		_____
up	_____	_____
		_____
out	_____	_____
		_____
put		
up with	_____	_____
		_____
someone down	_____	_____
		_____

12. Connect Your Class to the Real World

Every week, on your own or with a partner, find three expressions from the real world that are new to you. Keep an inventory in your notebook or on 3 x 5 cards, following the format in Appendix D, "Student Idiom Collection." Be ready to share what you found in small groups or with your entire class.

Crossword Puzzle for Lessons 1 and 2

Across

5. Don't wait for things to happen to you. Take the ____.
7. Come on. Tell me. Get it off your ____ .
9. Put ____ your hand. I have a surprise for you.
10. Weren't you put ____ when she said that?
11. In ____, I see now that I was wrong.
13. I ____ really taken aback when you said that.
14. Do you have the ____ to do it? I think it's scary.
16. Let's ____ it, OK? I don't feel like talking about it.

Down

1. He ____ off more than he could chew, and now he's under a lot of pressure.
2. Why do you look down ____ them?
3. I know you think it's easy. Don't rub ____ in.
4. ____ as not to bother anyone, they talked softly.
5. Relax. Let ____ slide.
6. You don't look happy. What's ____ you?
7. He said he wouldn't be ____ dead listening to that music.
8. Bite your ____ . Don't say things like that.
12. I need to ____ my pride and apologize to them.

18. Give it a ____ . You might be surprised to see that you'll do fine.
19. ____ bottom line is that no one can smoke in this building.
20. Now you're ____ . I agree with you 100%.
22. Come ____ think of it, I saw that movie a few years ago.
24. I can do ____ coffee, but not tea.

15. I know you're upset, but try to let it ____ .
17. I can see your ____ , but I still have a different opinion.
18. I have to ____ my pride and apologize to them.
21. Bite ____ tongue! How can you say such a thing?
23. ____ bottom line is that no one can smoke in the office.

In Class—Bored to Death or on the Edge of Your Seat?

Warm-Up

● Look at the title of this lesson and look at the cartoon. What do you think the two students are talking about?

● On the left, list three to five things that might make a class boring, and on the right, list three to five things that would make a class interesting:

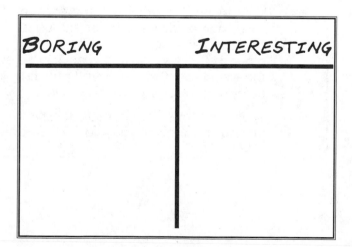

BORING | INTERESTING

Dialogue Steps

Choose one or more of the following:
(a)   Listen to the tape as you read the dialogue.
(b)   Say the dialogue in pairs.
(c)   Have two volunteers perform the dialogue in front of the class.

JAN: Mmm. This coffee is really strong.

STEVE: I like it that way.

JAN: So do I. All during my last class I was thinking about coming here and could almost taste the coffee.

STEVE: Sounds like it wasn't too exciting.

JAN: I was **bored to death**. I'm in that class only because it's a requirement, so I have to **stick it out**. The problem is, the professor doesn't know how to **spark our interest**. She just walks in and lectures. There's no discussion.

STEVE: **What a drag!** Don't people ask questions?

JAN: Oh, yeah, **once in a blue moon**. But I always see **an awful lot of** people doodling,* and I can tell their **minds are wandering**. Do you have any classes like that?

STEVE: I have only one big lecture class—world history—and the professor's the best. It's so interesting, I'm always **on the edge of my seat.** And when we have discussions, the room is filled with electricity.

JAN: I'm jealous. Too bad I already took history.

STEVE: You know, one day **it dawned on me** that I was lucky to be in her class because I found myself thinking about what she said for days after. Did you ever have a teacher like that?

JAN: I'd have to think about it. I don't know.

STEVE: You should come with me to class sometime, just to see what I mean.

JAN: Sounds like you're in love with her, Steve.

STEVE: Very funny. She could be my grandmother. Anyway, I guess what it really **comes down to** is her enthusiasm for the subject. She just loves history. I remember at the beginning of the semester I was **fooling around** a lot and not taking anything in school very seriously. I **bombed** the first history test, but then I **buckled down** because I started really enjoying school, especially her class.

JAN: You've got me really curious about this teacher. I think I'll **take you up on** your idea to visit your class. When does it meet?

exercise

---
*Drawing pictures in their notebooks.

Guess the Meanings

Below is a list of paraphrases of five of the idiomatic expressions contained in the dialogue. On your own or with a partner, try to guess the five.

Paraphrase	Idiomatic Expression from the Dialogue
1. How boring!	_____
2. failed	_____
3. accept	_____
4. I suddenly realized	_____
5. very rarely	_____

■ Understanding the New Expressions

Figure It Out with Others and/or On Your Own

(For more detailed instructions, see Lesson 1, page 3.)

WITH OTHERS:

Work in small groups to go through this information. The leader of each group should make sure that everyone participates equally.

ON YOUR OWN:

Read this entire section carefully.

For each expression circle the check mark or question mark in the margin to indicate whether or not you understand the information given.

All Clear?

√ ?

1. be bóred to déath

Definition: be extremely bored

Idiomatic Synonyms: **be bóred stíff; be bóred to téars**

S1: How was the movie?
S2: I **was bored to death.**

S1: The movie was three hours long and we **were bored stiff (bored to tears).**
S2: Why didn't you leave?
S1: 'Cause everyone else wanted to stay till the end.

√ ? 2. stick it óut

Definition: continue with something to the end, even if there are problems

S1: How are the winters in Alaska?
S2: Pretty tough. But we'll **stick it out** here for another two years.

S1: Come on, don't quit. You have only one more year of school.
S2: But I don't know if I can **stick it out.**

S1: It was a difficult marriage. They **stuck it out** until their children were out of the house, but then they got a divorce.
S2: That's a long time to wait, isn't it?

Contrast: **stick óut** = be especially visible in contrast to what is around

S1: What's that **sticking out of** your book?
S2: Oh—it's a twenty-dollar bill! I'm glad you saw it.

—Your shirt is **sticking out.** Tuck it in.
—Most people don't want to **stick out** in a crowd unless they want to attract attention.
—Everyone else was wearing white shirts. The child in the blue shirt **stuck out** and was embarrassed.

√ ? 3. spárk (someone's) ínterest (in)

Definition: create an unusual amount of interest (in something)

Note: A *spark* is a small, burning particle that is in a fire. It can blow in the wind and create another fire.

S1: Did you finish the book?
S2: You know, I really couldn't get into it. I tried, but somehow the topic didn't **spark my interest.**

—His teacher **sparked his interest in** space travel. That's all he talks about now.
—His teacher **sparked his interest in** learn**ing** about space travel.

√ ? 4. Whát a drág!

Definition: That's terrible! That's too bad! How boring!

Note: This expression is very informal, and its definition depends on the context of the conversation.

S1: After their car stereo was stolen, their house was robbed.
S2: What a drag!

S1: Yesterday I had two tests, today I have one, and tomorrow I have three.
S2: What a drag!

√ ? 5. ónce in a blúe móon

Definition: very rarely; not often

Origin: When a full moon occurs twice in a calendar month, the second moon is called a blue moon. This occurs very rarely.

Note: This expression is very informal.

S1: Do you ever hear from them anymore?
S2: Once in a blue moon.

S1: Don't you ever get a day off?
S2: Once in a blue moon.

√ ? 6. an áwful lót (of)

Definition: a lot of; a great deal of

Note: This is said for emphasis. It has nothing to do with the word *awful*, which has negative connotations.

—He made an **awful lot of** money in the stock market, didn't he?
—That teacher gives **an awful lot of** tests.
—You've been absent **an awful lot** lately, haven't you?

√ ? 7. someone's mínd is wándering

Definition: Someone is not paying attention and is thinking about different things.

Note: To *wander*, literally, is to walk around with no particular destination. When your mind wanders, it goes from one thought to another.

Pronunciation Note: Don't confuse the word *wonder* with *wander*. The *o* in *wonder* is pronounced like the *u* in the word *up*. The *a* in *wander* is pronounced like the *o* in the word *on*.

S1: Jan, I asked you a question. Didn't you hear me?
S2: I'm sorry. My **mind was wandering.**
S1: I know. You should be paying attention.

—My mind **wanders** every time I listen to him talk because he goes on and on.
—I was reading my book, but then I realized that **my mind was wandering** and I didn't remember anything I had read.

Contrast: **wander aróund (a place)** = walk around with no particular destination

—We **wandered around** the city for three hours. It was great.
—I think I'll **wander around** the museum for a while. Why don't we plan to meet at the station at 2:00?
—It doesn't matter where we go. Let's just **wander around**.

√ ? 8. be on the édge of one's séat

Definition: be extremely interested in something

Note: This is said when listening to or watching something.

—I **was on the edge of my seat** during the whole movie. And I was biting my nails.
—She **was on the edge of her seat,** listening attentively to every single word he said. If you had yelled "Fire," she wouldn't have heard you.

√ ? **9. it dáwned on someone (who, what, where, when, why, how, how much, how many, that)**

Definition: Someone suddenly thought of something.

Note: *Dawn* is the time of morning when the sun rises, when there is the beginning of light in the sky. When something *dawned on you*, some knowledge suddenly appeared out of the darkness.

Grammar Note: This expression usually occurs in the past tense.

—When I was reading the murder mystery, **it dawned on me who** did it.
—She was on the train when **it** suddenly **dawned on her what** she'd done. She immediately went back home and apologized to her husband.
—I was in the shower when **it dawned on me where** I had put all the money.
—In the middle of the night **it dawned on** the police officer **when** the guy had had the chance to commit the murders.
—At first I didn't understand, and then **it dawned on me why** you said that.
—Then it **dawned on him how** she stole the money. It was late at night, . . .
—When he saw her face, **it dawned on him how much** she cared.
—**It dawned on her how many** times the truth was right there in front of her, but she didn't see it.
—Last night **it dawned on them that** they needed to do something—fast.

√ ? **10. (Whát) it comes dówn to (is)**

Definition: The main point is . . . ,(This is said when there is a longer explanation but you want to say just your main point.)

Idiomatic Synonym: **boil dówn to (What it boils down to is . . .)**

Note: Think of boiling a sauce. Much of the liquid evaporates, but the main or most important part stays.

—I know you care a lot about your education. But **what it comes down to (what it boils down to)** is that you have to work hard to succeed.

S1: The police think he did it.
S2: Why?
S1: **It comes down to** the fact that he had a motive and was near the scene of the crime.

S1: She said she'd like to give me the job, but she can't.
S2: Why?
S1: **It boils down to** my not having enough experience.

√ ? 11. fool aróund (with)

Definition: do nothing constructive and nothing in particular; play

S1: What did you do during the summer?
S2: Nothing much. I just **fooled around with** my friends.
S1: What did you guys do?
S2: Oh, we went to the movies and the beach. Slept a lot.

—The two children were **fooling around** in the back of the classroom, and the teacher told them to pay attention.

Contrast: **fool aróund** = cheat on a husband or wife/have an affair

—He found out his wife was **fooling around** and now he wants a divorce.

√ ? 12. bómb

Definition: not do well; when said in relation to school, fail a test

—I didn't study, so I **bombed** my test.
—The play **bombed** in New York. The critics hated it.

√ ? 13. buckle dówn

Definition: start to work seriously

S1: You've been fooling around long enough. Now it's time to **buckle down** and get to work if you want to learn something.
S2: You're right. Starting right this minute I'm off to a new start.

Contrast: **buckle úp** = put on a seat belt

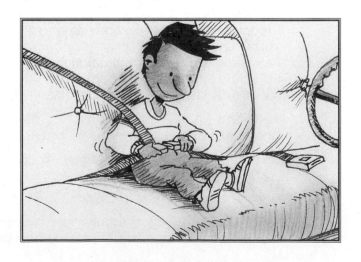

—I want everyone in the car to **buckle up** before we start, OK?

√ ? **14. take someone úp (on something)**

Definition: accept an invitation or an offer

S1: How about dinner tonight, and then a movie?
S2: That sounds great. I think I'll **take you up on** that.

S1: Where's Jan?
S2: Steve offered to take her to his history class, and she **took him up it.**

Exercises

1. Mini-Dialogues

Below are three exercises with two columns each, A and B. Column A contains the first lines of dialogues, and column B contains possible responses. For each opening line in column A, choose the *best* response from column B. Sometimes more than one response is possible. Not all responses can be used.

When checking the exercise in class, perform each mini-dialogue. One student should read an item from column A, and another student should respond with the answer from column B.

1. A

____ 1. How often do you read a book?
____ 2. I spent all weekend cleaning my apartment.
____ 3. Was the movie scary?
____ 4. What was his speech about?
____ 5. What it boils down to is that you fool around too much.

1. B

a. What a drag!
b. It sure was—I was on the edge of my seat for two hours.
c. No, I don't. I work hard.
d. Once in a blue moon.
e. I'll take you up on that.
f. I have no idea. My mind was wandering the whole time.

2. A

____ 1. Come on—just one more hour.
____ 2. An awful lot of people want to get into this movie.
____ 3. What sparked your interest in learning English?
____ 4. How was the show?
____ 5. How'd you do on your test?

2. B

a. Maybe you can stick it out, but I can't.
b. I bombed.
c. A lot of people were bored to death, but I loved it.
d. It's time to buckle down.
e. Movies, I guess.
f. I know—everyone is curious.

3. A

____ 1. It just dawned on me that we can try get that information on my computer.
____ 2. It comes down to this: either do the job or quit.
____ 3. They've really changed.
____ 4. What did you do when you got there?
____ 5. Did you find out what happened?

3. B

a. I know. Isn't it great? They decided to buckle down and work hard.
b. Yeah. It's a long story, but it boils down to one point.
c. It's sticking out.
d. We wandered around for a while, and then went out to dinner.
e. I guess I have no choice.
f. What a great idea!

2. Choosing the Idiom

The following is a review of a recent Hollywood movie. Fill in the blanks with the best possible expressions from the list. Pay special attention to how the expressions are used grammatically. You may need to consider verb tenses, subject-verb agreement, pronouns, active vs. passive voice, etc. Not all of the expressions in the list can be used. After you finish, practice reading the sentences aloud.

bored to death
fool around
What a drag
an awful lot
be on the edge of one's seat
it dawned on
buckle up

stick it out
stick out
once in a blue moon
mind is wandering
buckle down
come down to
take someone up on something

Last night I had the opportunity to see the kind of movie that comes out only (1) _____ . I went in thinking that I'd be (2) _____ , but I was completely surprised. It was terrific. The audience was so involved that no one was even eating popcorn. As for me, well, I (3) _____ for most of the movie.

Why was it so interesting? I'll tell you why. It was about what (4) _____ _____ of people care about—love and friendship. The heroine was married to a guy who didn't work. She tried and tried to get him to (5) _____ and go back to school and get a job. But no, he wouldn't. She didn't know what to do.

Then, one day she was sitting on her porch, thinking about her life. Her (6) _____ from one subject to another, when all of a sudden, (7) _____ her that she had the power to make a change in her life. She realized she didn't have to (8) _____ with this guy. (9) _____ _____ her life had been all these years.

Just at that moment her husband joined her on the porch and had a few of his own things to say. He asked her why she didn't work, why she (10) _____ in the house all day. Do you want to know how she responded? Well, folks, see the movie. You won't regret it.

3. Dictation

Your teacher or one of your classmates will read the dictation for this lesson from Appendix A, or you will listen to the dictation on the audio program. You will hear the dictation three times. First, just listen. Second, as you listen, write the dictation on a separate piece of paper. Third, check what you have written.

4. Pronunciation—Intonation in Statements

You stress words that carry the most information, usually nouns, main verbs, adjectives, and adverbs. But *one* of these words will carry the most meaning in each phrase, clause, or sentence, and that word, in addition to being stressed, should also be given the highest intonation (pitch). That word often contains *new* information for the listener.

Intonation, the rising and falling of your voice, helps you communicate meaning. High intonation communicates new information or what you think is most important, very high intonation communicates emotional feelings, and low intonation indicates that a sentence is ending. If you don't vary your intonation in English, you may give the impression that you are bored, and the people listening to you won't necessarily catch your meaning.

In the dialogue, Jan says, "This coffee is really strong."

If she wants to emphasize *really*, she will say: This coffee is **really** strong.

If she wants to emphasize *strong*, she will say: This coffee is really str-o-ng.*

Notice the three levels of intonation in these sentences:
high
normal
low

THE MOST COMMON INTONATION PATTERN IN STATEMENTS:

Phrases, clauses, and sentences usually end with rising + falling intonation on the last stressed word. Notice that the lowest intonation comes at the end of a sentence. (And keep in mind that words are stressed by making their stressed syllables longer.)

● If you want to know the tru-th,* I was bored to de-a-th.*

● I have to stick it o-u-t.*

● One day it **dawned** on me that I was lucky to be in her **class** because I found myself **thinking** about what she said for days af-ter.

You can change this pattern if you want to emphasize a word containing new, important information. That word does not have to be the last stressed word in a phrase, clause, or sentence:

1. I **like** it that way.

2. All during my last class I was thinking about coming here and could almost **taste** the cof-fee.

---

*The words *strong, truth, death* and *out* have only one syllable, but notice how you can lengthen them and move from high to low intonation to indicate the end of a phrase or sentence.

In sentence 1 above, *way* would usually be the last stressed word, but the speaker considers *like* more important. In sentence 2, the speaker wants to emphasize the new idea of *taste* more than the word *coffee*.

Practice 1

With a partner, say these sentences from the dialogue:

JAN: Mmm. This coffee is really str o ng.

STEVE: I like it that way.

JAN: So do I. All during my last class I was thinking about coming here and could almost taste the cof fee.

STEVE: Sounds like it wasn't too excit ing.

Practice 2

Practice using rising-falling intonation with the underlined words. These are the last stressed words in the phrases, clauses, and sentences. Notice that these words come right before commas, dashes, and periods. Remember to pause when you see these punctuation marks. (You will learn the rules for "question intonation" in the next lesson.)

JAN: I was bored to <u>death</u>. I'm in that class only because it's a <u>requirement</u>, so I have to stick it <u>out</u>. The problem <u>is</u>, the professor doesn't know how to spark our <u>interest</u>. She just walks in and <u>lectures</u>. There's no <u>discussion</u>.

STEVE: What a <u>drag</u>! Don't people ask questions?

JAN: Oh, yeah, once in a blue <u>moon</u>. But I always see an awful lot of people <u>doodling</u>.

STEVE: I have only one big <u>lecture</u> class—world <u>history</u>—and the professor's the <u>best</u>. It's so <u>interesting</u>, I'm always on the edge of my <u>seat</u>. And when we have <u>discussions</u>, the room is filled with <u>electricity</u>.

Practice 3

Practice using rising intonation with the underlined words. These words are *not* the last stressed words of phrases, clauses, or sentences. Instead, they are important words that focus on new information.

1. I can tell their <u>minds</u> are wandering.
2. I'm jealous. Too bad I already <u>took</u> history.
3. I guess what it <u>really</u> comes down to is her <u>enthusiasm</u> for the subject. She just <u>loves</u> history. I started really <u>enjoying</u> school, especially <u>her</u> class.
4. You've got me really <u>curious</u> about this teacher.

Practice 4

As you refer to the above information and exercises, underline or circle the words that you think should receive the highest intonation in the dialogue.

Practice 5: Listen and Speak

Listen again to the dialogue to see if the speakers' voices go up and down as you expected. Notice how the words with the most information to communicate are stressed and given higher intonation. Also notice how rising-falling intonation indicates the end of a phrase, clause, or sentence. Perform the dialogue with a partner, and if you can, record yourselves and compare your intonation to that of the speakers.

Practice 6: Pronunciation Review

Review the rules of Sentence Stress in Lesson 1. Then apply these rules to the movie review in Exercise 2 of this lesson, and underline or circle the words that should be stressed. You might also circle the words that should receive the highest intonation. Practice reading the movie review aloud.

5. Questions for Discussion and/or Writing

(For more detailed instructions, see Lesson 1, page 13.)

For Discussion: You can answer these questions orally in groups or in the *Walk and Talk* activity in Appendix B.

For Writing: You can write your own answers to these questions, or you can write the responses that you received from students during the *Walk and Talk* activity.

Questions

1. What are two or three things that bore you to death?
2. Think of a situation that you hated being in (perhaps a party, a wedding, a trip, a show, etc.). Did you stick it out to the end? Why or why not?
3. Which subjects that you have studied in school sparked your interest? Which didn't spark your interest?
4. What is something that you do only once in a blue moon? Why?
5. What kind of food do you like an awful lot? What kind of people do you like an awful lot? Why?
6. In what situations do you often find your mind wandering?
7. Everyone has had the experience of being on the edge of their seats at some kind of show, movie, or other type of performance. Describe one experience that you have had.
8. On vacation, when you have time to just fool around, what do you like to do?
9. Have you ever bombed a test? If yes, explain the circumstances.

6. Write Your Own

Here are some situations along with expressions from this lesson. Use your imagination and write your own sentences or dialogues to describe, explain, or act out the situations. Try to use at least two of the expressions in parentheses.

1. You do very well in school and want to learn how to play the guitar. However, you don't have a teacher. A classmate of yours who hasn't been doing very well in school offers to help you with the guitar if you help him or her with schoolwork. Write a conversation between you and your classmate in which you make plans to help each other. *(fool around, bomb a test, buckle down, it dawned on me, take someone up on something)*

A: _____

B: _____

_____

_____

_____

2. You are on the phone telling a friend about a party that you went to last week. You didn't know anyone there and didn't have a good time. Write what you say to your friend. *(be bored to death, what a drag, an awful lot of, come down to)*

_____

_____

_____

_____

_____

3. You stayed up very late last night and watched a horror film on TV. You were so scared that you almost turned the TV off, but you didn't. You watched the movie to the end. The next day you tell a friend about what you saw. Write what you say. *(be on the edge of one's seat, an awful lot, stick it out)*

_____

_____

_____

_____

_____

Choose one of your corrected "Write Your Own" sections and dictate it to a partner or group or your entire class. Before you do this, think about the pronunciation points you have studied and mark your sentences.

7. Scene Two

Consider the opening dialogue between Jan and Steve to be the first scene of a play. On your own, with a partner, or in a small group, write Scene Two (in other words, write a dialogue). Imagine that it is the following week and Jan has just visited Steve's world history class. They have coffee again and talk about the class.

As you write, see if any of the expressions from this or other lessons fit into the conversation. Also, feel free to use other expressions that you know. But don't feel that it is necessary to have an idiom in every sentence.

If possible, groups of students can practice various versions of Scene Two and then perform them for the class. You might even want to videotape these scenes.

8. Chain Story

Here is the beginning of a story. Continue the story by going around the room and having each student orally add a sentence, or get into small groups and have group members each add a sentence one by one. Try to have three to five expressions in your story. It will be helpful if the expressions from the dialogue are written on the board for all to see.

I was a pretty lazy kid in school . . . .

9. Role Playing

Using the new expressions from this lesson, act out the following role play. The new expressions should be written on the board.

Two students are walking on a college campus and talking about how their classes are going. They specifically talk about what they are studying and what they think of their teachers.

Possible starting line: *How are your classes this semester?*

10. Tic Tac Toe

In this variation of tic tac toe, to get an X or an O you need to create a grammatically correct sentence that is logical in meaning. Here is a game to start you off. Create as many games as you like, using expressions from Lesson 3. And if you would like to review expressions from any other lesson that you have studied, add them to the game.

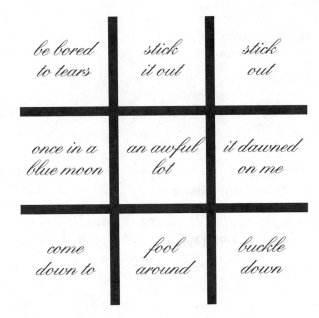

be bored to tears	stick it out	stick out
once in a blue moon	an awful lot	it dawned on me
come down to	fool around	buckle down

11. Expand on What You Now Know

In this lesson, you studied two-word verbs with the words *stick*, *take*, and *come*. Many more expressions exist in combination with these verbs.

You already know:

stick it out   **take** someone up (on)   **come** down to

To learn some more expressions with these verbs, with a partner ask a native speaker to help you fill out this chart. In order to do this kind of assignment, see Appendix C, "Contact Assignments," for information on how to start a conversation with a native speaker of English.

Pronunciation Note: Remember to stress the second part of two-word verbs.

	Meaning	Sample Sentence
stick		
up for someone	_____	_____
		_____
around	_____	_____
		_____
with	_____	_____
		_____
take		
something up with someone	_____	_____
		_____

over _____ _____

_____

down _____ _____

_____

after _____ _____

_____

come

down with something _____ _____

_____

up with something _____ _____

_____

up against something _____ _____

_____

12. Connect Your Class to the Real World

Every week, on your own or with a partner, find three expressions from the real world that are new to you. Keep an inventory in your notebook or on 3 x 5 cards, following the format in Appendix D, "Student Idiom Collection." Be ready to share what you found in small groups or with your entire class.

Homeless—Living from Hand to Mouth

Warm-Up

- In the circles, write down whatever words come to your mind when you hear the word "homeless." Then compile everyone's list on the board.

HOMELESS

- What do you think Victor Hugo meant when he said the following in 1862?

"Do not ask the name of a person who seeks a bed for the night. He who is reluctant to give his name is the one who most needs shelter."

Dialogue Steps

Choose one or more of the following:
(a) Listen to the tape as you read the dialogue.
(b) Say the dialogue in pairs.
(c) Have two volunteers perform the dialogue in front of the class.

HOMELESS MAN:	Hello, young man! What brings you to **this neck of the woods**?
REPORTER:	Actually, I was wondering if I could interview you for my newspaper.
HOMELESS MAN:	Me? About what?
REPORTER:	Well, we're doing a series of articles on the homeless, and I . . .
HOMELESS MAN:	And you want to know what happened to me, what I **live on,** what it's like to **live from hand to mouth** . . .
REPORTER:	Uh, yeah. I do want to know. Would you be willing to tell me your story?
HOMELESS MAN:	You got about three hours?
REPORTER:	Whatever we need.
HOMELESS MAN:	Well, go ahead and sit down.
REPORTER:	Thanks. Um, let's see, well, first I'd like to ask you . . .
HOMELESS MAN:	No questions. Just listen. You think I grew up poor, don't you? That I don't have an education. But you're **dead wrong.** I have a college degree. I worked for a big company. My parents **would turn over in their graves** if they could see me now.
REPORTER:	But how . . . ?
HOMELESS MAN:	I said, no questions. Just sit still and listen. In the beginning, I got up at 5 a.m. everyday and was at work by 7. And I stayed at the office till 8 in the evening. Thirteen hours! That was the only way I could **keep up with** all the work they **piled on** me. It just never **let up.** I never saw my family very much because when I got home, I usually went straight to bed. Well, I guess I was doing a pretty good job because I kept **moving up the ladder**. I became a manager and got more money, but I also had to work even more hours, and weekends, too. You can imagine that my wife never stopped complaining. She told me I was **getting burned out** and had no time for life.
REPORTER:	That must've been really hard to hear.
HOMELESS MAN:	Yeah, my marriage was **at stake**, so I went to my boss and asked for a vacation. He told me to wait three more months. He needed me there. So nothing changed. **Day in and day out** I worked and worked. Eventually my wife left. Can't say I blame her. And guess what? The company **closed down** a year later! I was left with nothing. I lost everything. Hey, how many hours do you work a day?

REPORTER:	Uh, . . .
HOMELESS MAN:	Just think about it. You know, I really **blew it**. I should have changed jobs. My family meant everything to me. But now I **get by**. I'm OK. I have some friends, some good times.
REPORTER:	Things could change, you know. You could start over. After all, you're educated.
HOMELESS MAN:	That's **wishful thinking,** young man.

Guess the Meanings

Below is a list of paraphrases of five of the idiomatic expressions contained in the dialogue. On your own or with a partner, try to guess the five.

Paraphrase	Idiomatic Expression from the Dialogue
1. absolutely incorrect	_____
2. made a big mistake	_____
3. in danger of failing	_____
4. this neighborhood	_____
5. stopped	_____

■ Understanding the New Expressions

Figure It Out with Others and/or On Your Own

(For more detailed instructions, see Lesson 1, page 3.)

WITH OTHERS:

Work in small groups to go through this information. The leader of each group should make sure that everyone participates equally.

ON YOUR OWN:

Read this entire section carefully.

For each expression, circle the check mark or question mark in the margin to indicate whether or not you understand the information given.

All Clear?

√ ? **1. in thís néck of the wóods**

Definition: in this area, in this place

Note: This expression contains a touch of humor and is used in a friendly way when a person is surprised to find someone in a certain place. The word THIS receives the most stress and highest intonation to show a contrast between *THIS* place and other places.

S1: What are you doing **in this neck of the woods**? I thought you moved away years ago.
S2: I did. I'm just visiting.

√ ? **2. líve on**

Definition: support oneself

S1: I have enough money to **live on** for a year without working.
S2: That's great. How did you manage that?

S1: She's **living on** unemployment insurance right now.
S2: Is it enough?

Contrast: **live ón** = continue to live; survive. (Notice the stress on the word on.)

—It's a tragedy that he died. But he will **live on** in our hearts.
—Classical music has **lived on** for centuries.

√ ? **3. líve from hánd to móuth**

Definition: have nothing; survive with whatever is available at the moment

Note: This is said about people who have no income at all.

S1: How do they manage?
S2: **They live from hand to mouth.** They do some panhandling (begging) and get their meals at soup kitchens.

Contrast: **líve from páycheck to páycheck** = make hardly enough money to last until the next check is received

—They have no savings. They just **live from paycheck to paycheck,** and it's hard. (Note that this expression is used to talk about people who do work but have trouble making enough money to last from one paycheck to another.)

√ ? 4. (be) déad wróng

Definition: (be) absolutely wrong

S1: If you think all the homeless are mentally ill, you're **dead wrong.**
S2: How do you know?
S1: I've talked to a lot of homeless people, and they are totally normal.

Contrast: **be déad against** = be absolutely against something

—I'm **dead against** going to that restaurant again. It's terrible.

√ ? 5. would turn (roll) óver in one's gráve

Definition: be very upset (This expression refers to what a dead person would do if he or she found out about something that he or she would strongly object to.)

Note: This expression is always used in a hypothetical sense, with *if* and *would.* After all, you cannot say that someone (really) turned over in his grave.

—If my grandfather saw me now (marrying someone of a different race or religion), he would **turn over in his grave.**
—If people who lived before 1900 could see the violence that's on TV and in the movies now, they **would roll over in their graves.**

√ ? 6. keep úp (with something or someone)

Definition: not fall behind

—To **keep up with** your work, you have to do your homework every night.
—If you can't **keep up,** then maybe you are in the wrong class.
—The little boy with short legs had trouble **keeping up with** the tall boys who were walking fast.
—It's great that you've **kept up with** so many technological advances.

Contrast: **catch úp (with)** = try to reach where one should already be

—If you don't keep up with your work now, you will have to **catch up** before the test.
—Go ahead. I'll **catch up** with you in a few minutes.
—I was absent for a week, but I **caught up** with all my work.

Contrast: **keep it úp** = continue

S1: I got an "A" on my test, Mom!
S2: Great! **Keep it up!** (or: **Keep up** the good work.)

√ ? 7. pile ón

Definition: give a lot of work

Grammar Note: As with other two-word verbs that can be separated, this expression takes these forms: pile on work

pile work on
  (someone)
pile it on (someone)

Notice that when a pronoun is used, it must be placed between the two words, not after them.

Pronunciation Note: The *i* in *pile* is pronounced like the word eye: /paɪl/.

S1: Boy, that teacher really **piles on** the work, doesn't he?
S2: He sure does. It's hard to keep up.

S1: Why did the boss keep **piling** all that work **on** you?
S2: I guess it's because I don't know how to say "no."

S1: She really **piles** it **on,** doesn't she?
S2: You can say that again!

√ ? 8. let úp

Definition: finally come to a stop after a great deal of pressure or a great quantity of something such as work or rain

Grammar Note: Past tense of *let* is *let;* no words can come between *let* and *up*

—The pressure finally **let up** after final exams.
—That teacher never **lets up.** We don't have time to breathe.
—If the rain **lets up,** let's go to the beach, OK?

Contrast: **let (someone) dówn** = disappoint someone

S1: I promise that I'll get the work done.
S2: Good. Don't **let me down.** I'm relying on you.

√ ? **9. móve (climb) up the ládder/move úp**

Definition: advance along a career path; move up/be promoted in a job

S1: How did you **move up the ladder** so fast?
S2: I guess I worked hard and know the right people.

Notice the stress change when you use the short form:
S1: How did you **move úp** so fast?
S2: I guess I worked hard and know the right people.

√ ? **10. gét burned óut**

Definition: become very tired, bored, and frustrated from doing the same work for too long (have no spark anymore, as in a fire that is going out)

—I'm **getting burned out.** I think I need to look for a different job. I've been doing this for twenty years.
—If you don't take a vacation soon, you're going to **get burned out.** You need a break.

Contrast: **be burned óut/burnt óut =** be without any vitality or life because of overwork or working at something for too long

S1: Why did he quit?
S2: He **was** really **burnt out**. But now he's got a completely new career and is feeling much much better.

Contrast: **búrnout** (noun) (Notice the stress change on the noun form.)

S1: Why did he quit?
S2: He was suffering from **burnout**. But now he's much better because he's in a new job.

√ ? 11. be at stáke

Definition: be at risk; be in danger of being lost

Spelling Note: Although they have the same pronunciation, *stake* and *steak* (meat) have entirely different meanings.

—You have to get a good lawyer to defend her. Her life is **at stake.**
—Your health is **at stake.** You have to quit smoking.
—My job is **at stake.** If I don't improve, I'm going to lose my job.

√ ? 12. day ín and day óut

Definition: every day

Note: This expression is used to emphasize the repetitiveness of something that is done every single day.

—I've been trying to help you **day in and day out,** but you don't listen to me.
—She's been working on a project **day in and day out,** and if she doesn't take a break soon, I don't know what's going to happen.

√ ? 13. close dówn

Definition: close a place permanently

—I went downtown to the department store where I usually shop and was shocked to see that it was **closed down.**
—The management threatened to **close down** the factory if there was a strike.
—The management threatened to **close** it **down.**
—The government plans to **close down** a lot of military bases.

√ ? 14. blów it

Definition: destroy an opportunity; fail

S1: She offered me a great job. I just hope that I don't **blow it.**
S2: You'll do fine. All you need is some confidence.

S1: **I blew it!** I had a chance to go to Disneyland with a few friends, but I wrote down the wrong date. They went last weekend!
S2: Relax. You'll have another chance to go someday.

√ ? **15. get bý**

Definition: manage to survive, but just barely

S1: Do you make enough money to live on?
S2: I **get by.** I have enough to buy food and pay my rent. But I don't go out very often.

√ ? **16. Thát's wíshful thínking.**

Definition: What you are saying is not likely to happen; you're being unrealistic.

S1: This lottery ticket is going to be a winner.
S2: **That's wishful thinking.**

S1: It's a holiday weekend. She won't give us homework.
S2: **That's wishful thinking.**

Exercises

1. Mini-Dialogues

Below are two exercises with two columns each, A and B. Column A contains the first lines of dialogues, and column B contains possible responses. For each opening line in column A, choose the *best* response from column B. Sometimes more than one response is possible. Not all responses can be used.

When checking the exercise in class, perform each mini-dialogue. One student should read an item from column A, and another student should respond with the answer from column B.

1. A

____ **1.** Did you know that minimum wage today is less than $6 an hour?
____ **2.** They think their kids are all going to become doctors and lawyers.
____ **3.** She was arrested for selling drugs.
____ **4.** Why do you work so much?
____ **5.** I can't believe how far behind I am in my work.
____ **6.** How did you do on the test?
____ **7.** I heard you lost your job.

1. B

a. That's wishful thinking!
b. Do you want me to help you catch up?
c. Her father would roll over in his grave if he knew.
d. How do people live on that?
e. Because I plan to move up the ladder really fast.
f. So many people live from hand to mouth.
g. I really blew it. I forgot everything!
h. That's right. My company closed down, and I'm not sure how I'm going to get by.

2. A

_____ 1. Why don't you want to take his class?
_____ 2. His life is at stake. He needs an operation immediately.
_____ 3. You're working so hard, you're going to get burned out before you're 30!
_____ 4. She just won't let up. Every day she talks about moving out.
_____ 5. Slow down! I can't keep up with you.
_____ 6. Did I really get an "A"?
_____ 7. I promise I'll help you. I won't let you down.

2. B

a. Don't worry about me. I know what I'm doing.
b. I heard he really piles on the work.
c. I know you won't. I can always rely on you.
d. Sorry. I'm always in a hurry.
e. You certainly did. Keep up the good work!
f. That must really upset her parents.
g. I'm dead against that.
h. Where do I sign to give permission?

2. Choosing the Idiom

Recently your friend had a terrible nightmare. Below is everything about it that she remembers. Fill in the blanks with the best possible expressions from the list. Pay special attention to how the expressions are used grammatically. You may need to consider verb tenses, subject-verb agreement, pronouns, active vs. passive voice, etc. Not all of the expressions in the list can be used. After you finish, practice reading the sentences aloud.

dead against	live on
at stake	let up
pile on	close down
dead wrong	day in and day out
keep up	get burned out
catch up	in this neck of the woods

Oh, it was terrible! At first, I was in a big classroom with around five hundred people. The professor kept (1) _____ the work. He wrote the homework assignment on the board—read five hundred pages in two days. He also gave us three lab reports to write and announced a big test. He just wouldn't (2) _____.
But the other students looked happy. I was the only one who seemed worried

about how to (3) _____.

    Then I remember I was in the library. I was trying to read all those pages. I was reading, but I couldn't remember anything, so I started to panic. Then, all of a sudden, my professor was sitting next to me. He asked me the strangest question: "What are you doing (4) _____?" I looked at him like he was crazy and told him that I was trying to do the work that he had assigned, and that I was upset because I couldn't remember anything I was reading. Then he asked me why I cared so much, and I told him that my grade was (5) _____. I needed an "A" in the class.

    He smiled when he heard this, and told me to close the book. He wanted to tell me what it was like when he was a student. (6) _____ _____ he studied and studied. But he never complained, and he never (7) _____. He never had to try to (8) _____ because he was never behind in his work. He told me that I went to too many movies and parties. I told him that he was (9) _____. I was a good student, but I was tired. He then asked me what the problem was—that he had assigned only fifty pages to read.

    That's when I woke up. What a relief to realize it was just a dream! But it seemed so real. I guess it shows that I'm under a lot of pressure these days.

3. Dictation

Your teacher or one of your classmates will read the dictation for this lesson from Appendix A, or you will listen to the dictation on the audio program. You will hear the dictation three times. First, just listen. Second, as you listen, write the dictation on a separate piece of paper. Third, check what you have written.

4. Pronunciation—Intonation in Questions

Information (Wh) Questions:

End with falling intonation. The last word that you want to stress should receive high intonation. After that, your voice will go down.

Yes-No Questions:

End with rising intonation.

Tag Questions:

These questions start out with a statement and end with a short yes-no question. Use falling intonation if you are quite sure of the response you will receive, if you are expecting the listener to confirm what you have said. Use rising intonation if you are unsure.

The following are questions from this lesson's dialogue.

Information Questions (Falling Intonation)

1. What brings you to ^{this} neck of the woods?

2. About $^{wh}a_{t?}$

3. And guess $^{wh}a_{t?}$

4. How many hours do ^{you*} work a day?

Yes-No Questions (Rising Intonation)

1. M$^{e?}$

2. Would you be willing to tell me your sto$^{ry?}$

3. You got about three ho$^{urs?}$

Tag Questions

(Falling Intonation)

(You expect confirmation of what you've said.)

You think I grew up ^{po}or, don't you?

(Rising Intonation)

(You really don't know the answer.)

You think I grew up ^{po}or, don't $^{you?}$

Practice 1

First, practice asking these questions with a partner. Then find the questions in the dialogue and write intonation arrows that show whether your voice should go up or down.

Practice 2: Listen and Speak

Listen to the dialogue again, and pay special attention to the intonation patterns used in questions. Perform the dialogue, giving special attention to question intonation.

Practice 3

Choose a dialogue from a lesson that you have already completed. Locate the questions and decide the kind of intonation they should receive. Write arrows that show whether your voice should go up or down. Then perform the dialogue with a partner.

---

*While it is true that pronouns are usually not stressed, they are stressed to show a contrast. For example: *I work eight hours a day. How many hours do YOU work?*

In the dialogue, the homeless man talks about how much he used to work and then asks the reporter, "How many hours do YOU work a day?" The emphasis on *you* shows the contrast between the two people.

Practice 4: Pronunciation Review

Review the rules for Intonation in Statements in Lesson 3. Then apply these rules to Exercise 2 of this lesson. Draw arrows on the words that should receive the highest intonation in both statements and questions. Practice reading Exercise 2 aloud.

5. Questions for Discussion and/or Writing

(For more detailed instructions, see Lesson 1, page 13.)

For Discussion: You can answer these questions orally in groups or in the *Walk and Talk* activity in Appendix B.

For Writing: You can write your own answers to these questions or you can write the responses that you received from students during the *Walk and Talk* activity.

Questions

1. Is there a minimum wage in your native country? Is it enough for people to live on?
2. Certain things and people live on even after their time has passed. For example, John Lennon of the Beatles was killed, but his music lives on. What other people or things live on and on?
3. Is it common for people you know to live from paycheck to paycheck, or do they actually save money?
4. Think of a relative of yours who has passed away (died). What is something happening today (personal, political, or social) that might cause that person to turn over in his or her grave?
5. As a student, do you generally keep up with your work, or do you always feel you are trying to catch up?
6. Have you ever had a teacher or boss who really piled on the work? If yes, how did you handle it?
7. If you were a teacher or boss, would you pile work on your students or employees? Explain.
8. What does a person need to do to move up the ladder in your native country? Are the opportunities to move up the same for men and women? Explain.
9. Do you know anyone who has worked too much day in and day out and then gotten burned out? If yes, explain the situation.

6. Write Your Own

Here are some situations along with expressions from this lesson. Use your imagination and write your own sentences or dialogues to describe, explain, or act out the situations. Try to use at least two of the expressions in parentheses.

1. You saw a movie about a big family that struggled during economically hard times. Write what you say to a friend about the movie. *(live on, live from hand to mouth, day in and day out, get by)*

_____

_____

_____

_____

2. You have a new job in a new city. You have a lot of work and are determined to impress your boss. You plan to be a big success. Write your thoughts. *(move up the ladder, keep up with, not blow this opportunity, not get burned out)*

_____

_____

_____

_____

3. A new teacher in a TV comedy is very nervous on the first day of school. He tells the students that they shouldn't be lazy and that they will learn a lot in the class because he will make them work hard. He isn't very friendly. Write what he says. *(don't let me down, be dead wrong, wishful thinking, pile on, not let up)*

_____

_____

_____

_____

Choose one of your corrected "Write Your Own" sections and dictate it to a partner or group or your entire class. Before you do this, think about the pronunciation points you have studied and mark your sentences.

7. Scene Two

Consider the opening dialogue between the homeless man and the reporter to be the first scene of a play. On your own, with a partner, or in a small group, write Scene Two (in other words, write a dialogue). What does the reporter say in response to the homeless man who thinks it's wishful thinking that he could start over again? Continue the conversation, with the reporter encouraging the homeless man.

As you write, see if any of the expressions from this or other lessons fit into the conversation. Also, feel free to use other expressions that you know. But don't feel that it is necessary to have an idiom in every sentence.

If possible, groups of students can practice various versions of Scene Two and then perform them for the class. You might even want to videotape these scenes.

8. Chain Story

Here is the beginning of a story. Continue the story by going around the room and having each student orally add a sentence, or get into small groups and have group members each add a sentence one by one. Try to have three to five expressions in your story. It will be helpful if the expressions from the dialogue are written on the board for all to see.

Once upon a time, there was a family that moved to a new city where they didn't know anyone. They were going to start over, after having had an unhappy experience where they used to live. . . .

9. Role Playing

Using the new expressions from this lesson, act out the following role play. The new expressions should be written on the board.

Two homeless people are sitting in the hallway of a subway station. They are telling each other their life stories.

Possible starting line: *You won't believe how good my life used to be.*

10. Tic Tac Toe

In this variation of tic tac toe, to get an X or an O you need to create a grammatically correct sentence that is logical in meaning. Here is a game to start you off. Create as many games as you like, using expressions from Lesson 4. And if you would like to review expressions from any other lesson that you have studied, add them to the game.

11. Expand on What You Now Know

In this lesson, you studied two-word verbs with the words *live, let, keep, catch, pile,* and *close.* Many more expressions exist in combination with these verbs.

You already know:
live on (continue to live)   **let** up
                                              down

keep up with   **catch** up with
pile on   **close** down

To learn some more expressions with these words, with a partner ask a native speaker to help you fill out this chart. In order to do this kind of assignment, see Appendix C, "Contact Assignments," for information on how to start a conversation with a native speaker of English.

Pronunciation Note: Remember to stress the second part of two-word verbs.

	Meaning	Sample Sentence
live		
up to	_____	_____
		_____
through	_____	_____
		_____
let		
someone in on something	_____	_____
		_____

keep

at it _____   _____

_____

off _____   _____

_____

catch

on _____   _____

_____

pile

up _____   _____

_____

close

up _____   _____

_____

off _____   _____

_____

12. Connect Your Class to the Real World

Every week, on your own or with a partner, find three expressions from the real world that are new to you. Keep an inventory in your notebook or on 3 x 5 cards, following the format in Appendix D, "Student Idiom Collection." Be ready to share what you found in small groups or with your entire class.

Crossword Puzzle for Lessons 3 and 4

Across

3. When the rain ____ up, let's go for a walk.

5. Stick ____ your hand. I have a surprise for you.

6. ____ in and day out, we work and work.

7. What it ____ down to is that we have no choice.

10. We don't make much money, but we ____ by.

Down

1. I ____ it! I bombed my test!

2. Come on, everyone. Stop ____ around and get to work!

4. My grade's at ____ . Can you help me after class?

7. It's time to ____ down and get to work.

8. What did you say? My mind was ____.

9. It was so exciting, we were on the ____ of our seats.

11. He moved up the ____ really fast, didn't he?
12. An ____ lot of people were there. It was very crowded.
14. Thanks. I think I'll take you ____ on that.
15. They are so poor that they live ____ hand to mouth.
19. Slow down, you guys! I can't ____ up with you.
20. Do you think we can live ____ $100 a month?
22. Don't give up. Can't you ____ it out for another few weeks?
25. You ____ up the ladder pretty fast, didn't you?
26. I spent all day cleaning my house. What a ____ .
27. It was so awful, I was bored to ____ .
29. What were you doing in that neck of ____ woods?
30. It just ____ on me that I should have been there.
31. I blew ____ ! I bombed my test!
32. That teacher really ____ on the work, doesn't she?

10. If they knew, they'd turn over in their ____ .
13. Are you all ____ up there in the back seat?
16. When I was unemployed, I lived from hand to ____ .
17. I'm really far behind. I have to catch up ____ my work.
18. Don't let ____ down. You made a promise.
21. We go there ____ in a blue moon.
23. When the store ____ down, a lot of people lost jobs.
24. They're dead ____ going. We have to go alone.
26. He's ____ wrong. I didn't say that.
28. Same as 4 down.
29. My job's at ____ if I can't learn to use this new computer.

Winning the Lottery— He's Got It Made

Warm-Up

1. a. Look at the cartoon and then read the dialogue silently to get the main idea. Don't worry about understanding the meanings of the new expressions.

   b. Imagine that you are going to change the title of this lesson. Instead of "He's Got It Made," what other title can you suggest?

   _____

   Your new title

   c. Compile a list of suggested titles on the board.

2. If there is a lottery in your native country, answer the following questions and give explanations:

   ● Do many people participate? Do you?

   ● Do winners get a lot of publicity?

   ● Is any money collected from the lottery sent to the school system or used in another way for the public?

Dialogue Steps

Choose one or more of the following:
(a) Listen to the tape as you read the conversation.
(b) Say the conversation in groups of three.
(c) Have three volunteers perform the conversation in front of the class.

JENNIE: **What's gotten into** Michael? What's he doing?

PETE: **I haven't the slightest idea.** Look, he's coming over to us.

MICHAEL: And these are for you.

JENNIE: What's the occasion?

MICHAEL: You haven't heard? I won the lottery last night. Ten million dollars!

JENNIE: Ten million dollars? Come on, **that's unheard of.** Are you sure?

MICHAEL: **Beyond the shadow of a doubt.** 6, 12, 22, 24, 25, and 28. I got every number. And it was the first time I ever bought a lottery ticket.

PETE: Beginner's luck, I guess. How do you feel?

MICHAEL: I'm in shock, **to say the least.** This is really all **beyond my comprehension.** It hasn't **sunk in** yet . . . maybe it never will.

JENNIE: Well, **I've got to hand it to you.** You sure look very calm. If I were in your shoes, I don't think I'd be able to stand still, **let alone** buy presents for people and have conversations with them.

MICHAEL: I'm not so calm. I really have no idea what's **in store** for me. You know, right now my whole life**'s up in the air.** I'm worried about **making the most of** this . . . I don't want all that money to **go down the drain.** I'm going to need some time to think.

PETE: Are you going to quit your job?

MICHAEL: I can't say yet. But I won't **rule it out.**

JENNIE: Well, you're right not to make any hasty decisions. And you know, you should **be on the lookout** for people who want to take advantage of you.

MICHAEL: I know. I plan to be very, very careful.

PETE: Well, no matter what you do, with ten million dollars, **you've got it made.**

Guess the Meanings

Below is a list of paraphrases of five of the idiomatic expressions contained in the conversation. On your own or with a partner, try to guess the five.

Paraphrase	Idiomatic Expression from the Dialogue
1. I really don't know.	_____
2. That doesn't happen.	_____

3. taking total advantage of   _____

4. you're a success   _____

5. What happened to   _____

■ Understanding the New Expressions

Figure It Out with Others and/or On Your Own

(For more detailed instructions, see Lesson 1, page 3.)

WITH OTHERS:

Work in small groups to go through this information. The leader of each group should make sure that everyone participates equally.

ON YOUR OWN:

Read this entire section carefully.

For each expression, circle the check mark or question mark in the margin to indicate whether or not you understand the information given.

All Clear?

√ ?

1. Whát's gotten ínto (someone)?

Definition: What has happened to (someone)?

Note: This is a question you might ask when you see that someone you know is acting in an unusual way.

Pronunciation Note: When you give the highest intonation to the last stressed word in this expression, this is what you say:

What's gotten into you?

S1: You haven't smiled all day. **What's gotten into** you?
S2: Nothing. I'm tired, that's all.

S1: I've never seen her so happy. **What's gotten into** her?
S2: I wonder. Let's go ask.

√ ?

2. nót háve (gót) the slíghtest ídea

Definition: not know at all

Synonyms: **háve nó idéa; nót háve a clúe**

Note: It is not possible to put this expression in the affirmative; you cannot say *I have the slightest idea.*

S1: Do you know what time it is?
S2: **I haven't (got) the slightest idea.** ⎤ I never wear my watch when I'm
　　　I have no idea. ⎬ on vacation.
　　　I don't have a clue. ⎦

S1: Do you think he knows about the surprise party?
S2: I'm sure he **doesn't have the slightest idea.** ⎤ We kept all the plans a
　　　　　has no idea. ⎬ secret
　　　　　doesn't have a clue. ⎦

Two other ways to emphasize that you don't know something:
"Béats mé!" and **"Yóur gúess is as góod as míne!"** (These
expressions are quite informal; you would use them only with
close friends or family members.)

S1: Do you know what time it is?
S2: **Beats me!**

S1: I wonder where they left the key.
S2: **Your guess is as good as mine.**

√ ? 3. Thát's unhéard of

Definition: That's unbelievable; that never happens.

Note: This is said when something is so unusual that it is not
"heard of."

S1: In some countries, students go to school on Saturdays.
S2: **That's unheard of** here.

S1: They're paid only $2 an hour.
S2: **That's unheard of.** How awful!

√ ? 4. beyond the shádow of a dóubt

Definition: absolutely sure/certain, with no doubt at all

Note: Some people say "beyond *a* shadow of a doubt."

S1: Are you sure? Is she really pregnant?
S2: Yes. **Beyond the shadow of a doubt.**

—In the U.S. legal system, a person is considered innocent unless proven guilty **beyond the shadow of a doubt.**

√ ?   **5. to sáy the léast**

Definition: to say the minimum

Note: This is said when it is possible to say more.

S1: I work eight hours a day, go to school three hours a day, and have two young children. I'm tired, **to say the least.**
S2: You should be.

—We have great jobs and a nice place to live. We're very lucky, **to say the least.**

√ ?   **6. beyond one's comprehénsion (that)**

Definition: outside one's ability to understand

Note: This is said when it is very hard or impossible to believe/ understand something.

—I find calculus **beyond my comprehension.** Perhaps it's because I never learned algebra well.
—It's **beyond my comprehension that** so many people can live in such a small area.
—Nobody can believe that she committed the crime. It's **beyond our comprehension that** she could break the law.

√ ?   **7. sink ín**

Definition: be gradually believed or understood

Note: When something sinks in the water, it typically goes down slowly. When information that is difficult to understand or believe enters the brain, it "sinks in" slowly until it is clearly understood.

—When they heard the news that the war was over, they didn't believe it at first. It took time for the news to **sink in.**

S1: You're married? But you're only 18!
S2: Uh-huh. We got married last week.
S1: I've got to sit down and let this **sink in.** I don't believe it.

S1: Maybe after I study this for six hours or so it'll all **sink in.**
S2: It'd better. The test is tomorrow.

Other Expressions with "Sink":

one's héart sánk = something happens to make a person lose hope and become very disappointed. This expression is used in the past tense.

—**My heart sank** when I heard the news about the election. My candidate lost.
—Her mother's **heart sank** when she heard that her daughter was getting a divorce.

sínk or swím = fail or be successful; learn without being taught or trained; the image here is that if someone who doesn't know how to swim is thrown into the water, he or she will have to work hard to learn to swim, or otherwise "sink" (drown).

—Immigrant children who start school without any English classes have to **sink or swim.**
—When she started her new job, no one trained her. It was a **sink or swim** situation. (In this sentence, *"sink or swim"* is used as an adjective to describe the word *situation*.)

have a sínking féeling that = have a terrible feeling in one's stomach that something terrible has happened, is happening, or will happen

—**I have a sinking feeling that** right now Ruth is waiting for me at the wrong airport.
—**I have a sinking feeling that** he's going to be sorry that he took that job.
—**She has a sinking feeling that** Jon heard what she said about him yesterday.

√ ? 8. I've gót to hánd it to you.

Definition: I have to give (you) credit for something; you did a good job.

Pronunciation Note: When you give the highest intonation to the last stressed word, you say:

I've got to ↱ hand it to ↘ you.

—**I've got to hand it to you.** You managed to get all your work done on time, and I know you were sick.
—**I've got to hand it to you.** You won all that money in the lottery, but you didn't change. You're still the great person you always were.

√ ? **9. lét alóne**

Definition: It is certainly impossible to. . . . Someone certainly can't/won't. . . .

Note: This is said as a strong negative response to a question or suggestion. Here is the typical conversational pattern with this expression:

A: Why don't you X?
B: We can't Y (Y is easier to do than X), **let alone** X.

A: Why don't you fly to Mexico?
B: We can't afford to drive, **let alone** fly.

Easier thing to do	*Harder thing to do*
—I can't walk fast,	**let alone** run.
—It's difficult to speak English,	**let alone** write essays.
—I can't speak English,	**let alone** understand the culture.
—I don't want to take a walk,	**let alone** climb that mountain.

Contrast: **léave (someone or something) alóne** = stay away from

—Please **leave me alone.** I don't feel like talking right now. (This might be said to someone you know very well.)
—**Leave** my papers **alone.** I don't want anyone to touch them. (Because this is a command, it is not very polite.)

√ ? **10. be in stóre (for someone)**

Definition: be waiting to happen in the future

S1: There**'s** a surprise **in store for** you when you get home.
S2: What is it?
S1: I'm not going to tell you. You just have to wait!

S1: (Mom) You know what**'s in store** when you misbehave, don't you?
S2: I know.
S1: Now play quietly or you'll have to go to your room.

S1: There are going to be some big changes around here soon.
S2: Do you know what**'s in store fo**r me?
S1: I'm afraid you might lose your job.

√ ? **11. be úp in the aír**

Definition: be undecided

S1: Are you going to take the new job and move?
S2: We're not sure. Everything**'s up in the air.** There's a chance we might stay here if I can get a higher salary.

S1: When's the wedding?
S2: I don't know. Now they're saying they're not going to get married, that they're just going to live together. It**'s** all **up in the air.**
S1: Their parents must love that. (This is a sarcastic remark; the speaker means exactly the opposite of what he or she is saying.)

√ ? **12. máke the móst of (something)**

Definition: get the most from something; take advantage of something

S1: We have one more day here, and we're going to **make the most of** it. We're going to eat at the best restaurant and walk around all night.
S2: Aren't you going to sleep?
S1: No way. We want to take advantage of every second. Who knows? We may never come back!

S1: Do you think this is the wrong day for the party?
S2: It must be—there's no one here. But since we've driven so far, let's **make the most of** it and look around town before we go back home.

√ ? **13. go dówn the dráin**

Definition: be wasted

Note: When something *goes down the drain,* it is lost.

—The electricity went out, and I didn't save my work on the computer. All those hours of work **went down the drain.**
—They won a few hundred dollars at the casino, but it all **went down the drain** because they lost it the next day.

√ ? **14. rule (something or someone) óut**

Definition: say that something is impossible or that it can't happen

Origin Note: This expression probably comes from drawing a line through written material with a ruler.

S1: Dad, can't we go to Disneyland?
S2: Maybe. I won't **rule it out,** but there are other places we're thinking of for vacation.

—It's too dangerous to travel there, so we have to **rule it out.**
—The doctor won't **rule out** a broken bone until he's seen an X-ray.
—The police arrested someone yesterday, but then they **ruled her out** because the witness didn't identify her.

√ ? **15. be on the lóokout (for)**

Definition: be constantly looking carefully for someone or something

—Airport officials **are** always **on the lookout for** any suspicious packages or people.

—We'**re on the lookout for** people who can do some good translations. Will you let us know if you know anyone?

—It's important to **be on the lookout for** fires during the summer.

√ ? **16. háve gót it máde/háve it máde**

Definition: be sure of success

S1: He'**s got it made.** (or: He **has it made.**) He has a great job, a great girlfriend, and. . . .

S2: Are you jealous?

S1: You think all those famous stars **have (got) it made,** don't you? Well, you know, not all of them are so happy. Look at the number of divorces.

S2: You may have a point.

—These days, if you've got a good education, know computers, and speak a few languages, **you've got it made.** You'll have no trouble finding a job.

Exercises

1. Mini-Dialogues

Below are three exercises with two columns each, A and B. Column A contains the first lines of dialogues, and column B contains possible responses. For each opening line in column A, choose the *best* response from column B. Sometimes more than one response is possible. Not all responses can be used.

When checking the exercise in class, perform each mini-dialogue. One student should read an item from column A, and another student should respond with the answer from column B.

1. A

_____ 1. I don't believe it! Are you sure?
_____ 2. You look really upset. What happened?
_____ 3. I'm on the lookout for a good used car.
_____ 4. I have a sinking feeling that I got a lousy grade on that test.
_____ 5. When's our next test?

1. B

a. I lost my homework. All my work went down the drain.
b. What makes you think so?
c. It's a sink or swim situation.
d. Uh-huh. Beyond the shadow of a doubt.
e. I'll keep my eyes open. If I see one, I'll call you.
f. Beats me!

2. A

_____ 1. The teacher wants us to read a whole book over the weekend.
_____ 2. That was incredible news, wasn't it?
_____ 3. Are they going to send soldiers in?
_____ 4. Are they going to move?
_____ 5. Nice car. Looks like you've really got it made.

2. B

a. Maybe. The president hasn't ruled that out.
b. Really? That's unheard of!
c. I'm doing OK.
d. Not yet. Everything's up in the air till they hear about that job.
e. Just try to make the most of it.
f. I know. It hasn't sunk in yet. I may never believe it.

3. A

_____ 1. It's so hot, it's hard to think, let alone work.
_____ 2. Wait till you hear what we have in store for you!
_____ 3. I've got to hand it to you. You handled that situation very well.
_____ 4. It's absolutely beyond my comprehension that they could do that.
_____ 5. I don't have the slightest idea about what happened last night.

3. B

a. Why don't we take a break?
b. Thanks, I tried, and it wasn't easy, believe me.
c. Neither do I.
d. I know what you mean. I don't know what's gotten into them.
e. It sure sounds like it's going to be something special.
f. To say the least, I think it's a great idea.

2. Choosing the Idiom

The following is a letter that Michael, the lottery winner, has received from his mother. She lives in another city in a small apartment. She is a widow, and has never had much money. For most of her adult life she worked very hard to make sure that her son had a good education so that he could get a good job.

Fill in the blanks with the best possible expressions from the list. Pay special attention to how the expressions are used grammatically. You may need to consider verb tenses, subject-verb agreement, pronouns, active vs. passive voice, etc. Not all of the expressions in the list can be used. After you finish, practice reading the sentences aloud.

What's gotten into _____ ?	not have the slightest idea
unheard of	beyond the shadow of a doubt
to say the least	beyond _____ comprehension
sink in	have a sinking feeling
let alone	be in store
be up in the air	make the most of
go down the drain	rule out
be on the lookout	have got it made

Dear Michael,

I still don't believe your news. I don't know if it will ever (1)_____

_____. I saw you on TV tonight and am very happy for you,

(2)_____ _is say in lease _____. You looked so happy and healthy!
That's all a mother can want.

The phone hasn't stopped ringing. Everyone is sending their congratulations.

At this point, I can hardly think, (3)____ let alone _____ _____ write, but
I'm going to try to write because a lot of thoughts are jumping around in my
mind and I need to get them down.

I have to admit, I'm worried about you. Right now, you think that you

(4)__ have got it made _____, but where will you be a year from now?

You have to be extremely careful. I (5)_ have a saying feeling ____ that
there will be people around you who will try to take your money. You need to

constantly (6)_____, or all that money can

(7)_____.

You know, I've always said that money doesn't make people happy.

Remember that. It's not (8)__ unheard of _____ for some very
rich people to have very unhappy lives. I don't want that to happen to you.

I want you to (9)__ make the most _____ this time in your life.
Pay all your bills, and take a trip. Enjoy yourself. I don't want anything. Find
yourself a nice woman to marry, but make sure that she isn't after your money.
Please promise me that you won't get married until you are convinced

(10)__ beyond the shadow of a doubt _____ that the woman isn't a fortune hunter.

You said that your plans (11)_____. But
please let me know what you decide to do. And find out how much you will
have to pay in taxes. I'm sure you will be shocked. And don't forget to give a
nice amount of money to charity. You should share your wealth.

Well, I guess we can't really know exactly what (12) _was in store_

_____, can we? I just wish you well. Don't let all this money change you,

Michael.

LOTS OF LOVE,

Mom

3. Dictation

Your teacher or one of your classmates will read the dictation for this lesson from Appendix A, or you will listen to the dictation on the audio program. You will hear the dictation three times. First, just listen. Second, as you listen, write the dictation on a separate piece of paper. Third, check what you have written.

4. Pronunciation Part 1—Thought Groups

Look at the following from the dialogue:

MICHAEL: (I'm in shock,) (to say the least.) (This is really all beyond my comprehension.) (It hasn't sunk in yet. . .) (maybe it never will.)

JENNIE: (Well,) (I've got to hand it to you.) (You sure look very calm.) (If I were in your shoes,) (I don't think I'd be able to stand still,) (let alone buy presents for people) (and have conversations with them.)

Notice the groups of words in parentheses. Each group expresses a thought. By saying each group of words without pausing between the words, we create a certain rhythm.

At the end of each thought group our voices go down in pitch and we sometimes pause briefly.

If you say each word equally with pauses between them, you won't be using English rhythm. This can make your English difficult to understand, even if you are using clear pronunciation of sounds and correct grammar and vocabulary.

Question: How can you know what words make up a thought group?

Answer: What goes into a thought group can vary, so it's not possible to give rules for 100% of the time. But you can follow these general guidelines:

What may be a thought group	**Example**
• a short sentence	_(I've got to hand it to you.)_
• a phrase	_(to say the least)_
• a clause	_(If I were you,)_
• transition words	_you know, well, first, next, finally_

In writing, commas, periods, and other punctuation marks indicate the ends of thought groups. These markers help make written language more comprehensible to us. In speech, changes in pitch and short pauses make our spoken language more comprehensible to our listeners.

Practice 1

Put parentheses around the thought groups in the dialogue. Don't be afraid to guess. Say the words in the thought groups to yourself to see if they feel naturally grouped.

Example:

You don't say: (What's) (gotten) (into) (Michael?)   (What's) (he) (doing?)
You say: (What's gotten into Michael?)   (What's he doing?)

Pronunciation Part 2—Linking

As you know from Lesson 2, linking means connecting. In English we often link words when one word ends in a consonant sound and the next word starts with a vowel sound. The same happens when a word ends in a vowel sound and the next word starts with a consonant sound.

We also link words when the final sound of one word is the same as the beginning sound of the next word, such as the *first time.*

We link words within thought groups, and that may be one reason why you may not always understand what you hear but are able to understand the same words when they are written. Here are some examples of linked words within thought groups:

(What's gotten into Michael?)

(What's 'e doing?)

(Come on.) (That's unheard of.)

(. . . have conversations with them)

The Silent "h"

Notice in the second example above that the *h* in the word *he* is dropped, so the *s* sound at the end of *What's* is linked with the vowel sound *e.* In spoken English it is common for the *h* to be dropped in the pronouns *he, his, her,* and *him*:

Full word	Reduced (shortened) word
he	'e
his	'is
her	'er
him	'im or 'em

Sounds vs. Spelling

Be careful not to confuse letters from the alphabet and actual sounds. When you are linking words, look at and listen for the sounds rather than the letters.

Look at the word *university.* It starts with the vowel letter *u,* but the first sound in this word is really /y/. Also look at the word *hour.* It starts with the consonant letter *h,* but the first sound in this word is really the vowel /aʊ/. And don't let words that end in silent vowels fool you. The last *letter* in the word *whole* is *e,* but the last *sound* is really /l/.

Two of the Same Consonant Sound

Within thought groups, when one word ends in a consonant sound and the next word starts with the same sound, link the two words by pronouncing the consonant sound only once.

Two Words	How They Sound When Linked	
It was the first time I ever bought a lottery ticket. I've got to hand it to you.	firs-time	/fɑrs·táɪm/
	go-da*	/gɑ·də/
. . . let alone buy presents for people and have conversations with them.	wi-them	/wɪ́ðəm/
Right now my whole life's up in the air. You're right not to make any hasty decisions.	ho-life's	/hóʊ.láɪfs/
	yo-right	/yɔ.ráɪt/
Be on the lookout for people who want to take advantage of you.	wanta *or* wanna	/wɑ́ntə/ /wɑ́nə/

Practice 2

Go back to the dialogue and insert linking lines between the words within the thought groups. Practice saying the thought groups aloud again, but this time also focus on linking.

Practice 3: Listen and Speak

Listen again to the dialogue. Pay special attention to how the speakers create thought groups. Notice that they don't say words individually. Also listen for words that are linked together. If you can, record yourself and compare your pronunciation to the pronunciation on the tape.

Practice 4: Pronunciation Review

Review the rules for stress and linking in two-word verbs in Lesson 2. Then, in any of the dialogues in Lessons 3, 4, or 5, apply these rules to the two-word verbs you have learned. Circle the words that should receive the most stress, and draw linking lines where necessary.

5. Questions for Discussion and/or Writing

(For more detailed instructions, see Lesson 1, page 13.)

For Discussion: You can answer these questions orally in groups or in the *Walk and Talk* activity in Appendix B.

For Writing: You can write your own answers to these questions or you can write the responses that you received from students during the *Walk and Talk* activity.

Questions

1. What is Michael's mother (in Exercise 2) worried about? Re-read her letter, and make a list of her concerns about his sudden wealth. Add any concerns that you might have.

---

*See note at the bottom of page 31.

2. Think of a friend or relative whose behavior seemed to suddenly change (becoming very happy or depressed). Did you say something to anyone equivalent to the expression "What's gotten into him/her?" Explain the circumstances.

3. What are some American customs that are unheard of in your native country? What are some customs in your native country that are unheard of in the U.S.?

4. Describe some news that you once heard that took time to sink in. (This would be news that was a good or bad shock, that was hard to believe at first.)

5. Do foreign children ever attend schools in your native country? If yes, are they given language classes, or are they expected to enter regular classes and "sink or swim"?

6. Complete these three sentences with the expression *let alone:*

   a) I can't _____ , let alone_____.

   b) It's difficult to _____ , let alone_____.

   c) I don't want to _____ , let alone_____.

7. What do you think is in store for you after you finish studying English?
8. What aspects of your life are up in the air?
9. Describe a time when your efforts to do something went down the drain.
10. Describe the life of someone (real or imaginary) who's got it made.

6. Write Your Own

Here are some situations along with expressions from this lesson. Use your imagination and write your own sentences or dialogues to describe, explain, or act out the situations. Try to use at least two of the expressions in parentheses.

1. Someone you knew many years ago in school is now a politician who has just won an election. You and a friend of yours find this hard to believe because this politician was never very popular in school. You talk to your friend about how surprised you are and about how you don't know what to expect in the future. Write the conversation between you and your friend. *(beyond one's comprehension, sink in, be in store)*

A: _____

B: _____

_____

_____

_____

2. Your friend is talking about how she felt when she lost her job. When she went to work one day, she had no idea what would happen. Losing her job came as a big surprise, and she got very upset. But she explains that she's better now, and looking for a new job. Write what she tells you. *(not have the slightest idea, heart sank, down the drain, be up in the air, be on the lookout for)*

_____

_____

_____

_____

_____

3. Your friend is selling everything he owns to make money to travel around the world for at least a year. He asks you to help him sell his stuff. You are very surprised, and talk to him. Write what you say. *(what's gotten into you, to say the least, unheard of, let alone, I've got to hand it to you)*

_____

_____

_____

_____

Choose one of your corrected "Write Your Own" sections and dictate it to a partner or group or your entire class. Before you do this, think about the pronunciation points you have studied and mark your sentences.

7. Scene Two

Consider the opening conversation of Jennie, Pete, and Michael to be the first scene of a play. On your own, with a partner, or in a small group, write Scene Two, using Michael and *one* of the other characters (in other words, write a dialogue). Imagine that it is a month later, and Michael is telling the other person about some decisions he has made about his life.

As you write, see if any of the expressions from this or other lessons fit into the conversation. Also, feel free to use other expressions that you know. But don't feel that it is necessary to have an idiom in every sentence.

If possible, groups of students can practice various versions of Scene Two and then perform them for the class. You might even want to videotape these scenes.

8. Chain Story

Here is the beginning of a story. Continue the story by going around the room and having each student orally add a sentence, or get into small groups and have group members each add a sentence one by one. Try to have three to five expressions in your story. It will be helpful if the expressions from the dialogue are written on the board for all to see.

One day, _____ (someone from your class) was hiking in gold country in California and discovered gold. . . .

9. Role Playing

Using the new expressions from this lesson, act out the following role play. The new expressions should be written on the board.

Two people are "panning for gold" in gold country in California, and suddenly one of them finds a piece of gold, called a nugget. This is a very big nugget, and she is very excited because this may mean that they will become very wealthy.

Possible starting lines: Look! There's gold in here. We're rich!!!

10. Tic Tac Toe

In this variation of tic tac toe, to get an X or an O you need to create a grammatically correct sentence that is logical in meaning. Here is a game to start you off. Create as many games as you like, using expressions from Lesson 5. And if you would like to review expressions from any other lesson that you have studied, add them to the game.

11. Expand on What You Now Know

In this lesson, you studied two-word verbs with the words *sink* and *rule*. Many more expressions exist in combination with these verbs.

You already know:

sink in   **rule** out

To learn some more expressions with these words, with a partner ask a native speaker to help you fill out this chart. In order to do this kind of assignment, see Appendix C, "Contact Assignments," for information on how to start a conversation with a native speaker of English.

Pronunciation Note: Remember to stress the second part of two-word verbs.

	Meaning	Sample Sentence
sink		
one's teeth into something	_____	_____
		_____
(back) into a chair	_____	_____
		_____
rule		
against (legal meaning)	_____	_____
		_____
on (legal meaning)	_____	_____
		_____
over (political meaning)	_____	_____
		_____

12. Connect Your Class to the Real World

Every week, on your own or with a partner, find three expressions from the real world that are new to you. Keep an inventory in your notebook or on 3 x 5 cards, following the format in Appendix D, "Student Idiom Collection." Be ready to share what you found in small groups or with your entire class.

Stuck in an Elevator— Cooped Up and Sitting Tight

Warm-Up

How have you reacted, or how would you react, in an emergency situation? Complete this chart and then discuss your responses with others in your class.

Possible responses

- panic (sweat, breathe fast, faint, scream, cry)
- keep calm (not do the above)
- be nervous but not panicked

Emergency Situation	If you have experienced this, what did you do?	If you haven't experienced this, what do you think you would do?
a. stuck in an elevator for two hours	_____	_____
b. a strong earthquake	_____	_____
c. a big flood	_____	_____

d. a strong hurricane _____ _____

e. a violent tornado _____ _____

f. other: _____ _____ _____

Dialogue Steps

Choose one or more of the following:
(a) Listen to the tape as you read the dialogue.
(b) Say the dialogue in pairs.
(c) Have two volunteers perform the dialogue in front of the class.

MR. CLAUSTROPHOBIA*:	Oh, no! This can't be happening.
MRS. CALM:	Hmm. Well, that certainly happened **out of the blue**. I wonder what's going on.
MR. CLAUSTROPHOBIA:	I'm going to ring the alarm. **This is the last straw.** I told them weeks ago to check this elevator. I would have **been better off** taking the stairs.
MRS. CALM:	Do you mean this has happened before?
MR. CLAUSTROPHOBIA:	It sure has. It was a few weeks ago, but I wasn't in the elevator . . . Oh, if I'**m cooped up in** here really long, I don't know what I'm going to do. I'**m** already **at the end of my rope.**
MRS. CALM:	Well, **for crying out loud,** young man, don't **lose your head.** Just calm down, and I'm sure they'll get this thing started again as soon as they can.
MR. CLAUSTROPHOBIA:	You know, I **knocked myself out** to be on time for my meeting, and now look.
MRS. CALM:	Complaining isn't going to help. We'll just have to **make do** here, and be thankful that we have some light and some company.
MR. CLAUSTROPHOBIA:	Actually, you're right. I'm glad I'm not alone in here, or I'd be **climbing the walls.**
MRS. CALM:	So, you see—it could be a lot worse. Just please do me a favor and **keep a level head.** Let's just **sit tight** and wait for help.
MR. CLAUSTROPHOBIA:	How can you be so calm? It sounds like you've been stuck in elevators before!
MRS. CALM:	Well, the truth is, this is my first time. But why should I panic? What good would it do? I don't want to **dwell on** things that scare me. I'd rather pass the time in here pleasantly.
MR. CLAUSTROPHOBIA:	How would that ever be possible?

_____
*Claustrophobia is the fear of being in enclosed or small spaces.

MRS. CALM:	Hmm, we could tell each other our life stories. Who knows, we might even **come through** this as friends!
MR. CLAUSTROPHOBIA:	Huh?
MRS. CALM:	We can help each other by doing something that'll distract us. Why don't you just sit down and tell me about yourself?

Guess the Meanings

Below is a list of paraphrases of five of the idiomatic expressions contained in the dialogue. On your own or with a partner, try to guess the five.

Paraphrase	Idiomatic Expression from the Dialogue
1. go crazy	_____
2. with no warning	_____
3. be patient	_____
4. stuck in	_____
5. think too much about	_____

■ Understanding the New Expressions

Figure It Out with Others and/or On Your Own

(For more detailed instructions, see Lesson 1, page 3.)

WITH OTHERS:

Work in small groups to go through this information. The leader of each group should make sure that everyone participates equally.

ON YOUR OWN:

Read this entire section carefully.

For each expression, circle the check mark or question mark in the margin to indicate whether or not you understand the information given.

All Clear?

√ ?   **1. óut of the blúe**

Definition: suddenly, from nowhere, without any warning

Synonym: **óut of nówhere**

S1: .**Out of the blue,** she told him that she was leaving. (Or: She told him she was leaving **out of the blue.**)

S2: I bet he was shocked.

—She was speeding, but there was no one else on the road. Then, **out of the blue,** a police car came out of the trees and went after her with its sirens blaring. She was terrified.

Other Expressions with "out of"

óut of the córner of one's éye = see something indirectly
—When he was getting money from the ATM, he saw a strange person out of the corner of his eye, so he got scared.
óut of hánd = disorganized, chaotic, out of control
—The party started to get out of hand when some people got drunk.

√ ? 2. the lást stráw

Definition: the last one of a series of frustrating things that have happened

Note: This last event makes a person lose all patience.

Origin: This is a shortened version of the expression *the straw that broke the camel's back*. The origin of this expression, according to the *Morris Dictionary of Word and Phrase Origins*, is from the writing of Charles Dickens: "'As the last straw breaks the laden camel's back,' meaning that there is a limit to everyone's endurance, or everyone has his breaking point. Dickens was writing in the nineteenth century and he may have received his inspiration from an earlier proverb, 'Tis the last feather that breaks the horse's back.'"

—They've been late every time we've invited them to the movies, and now we're going to miss the beginning. **This is the last straw.** I'm never inviting them again.
—Do you hear those drums upstairs? I've asked them over and over again to practice before 10, and it now it's 11. **This is the last straw.** I'm going to call the police.

√ ? **3. be bétter off**

Definition: be in a better state or condition

Opposite: **be wórse off**

Grammar Note: These expressions are often followed by gerunds.

Pronunciation Note: Stress the word *off* when it comes at the end of a sentence.

S1: Wouldn't you **be better off** fly**ing** rather than driving?
S2: But I want to see the sights on the way. I'm in no hurry.

—We're the first generation to **be worse off** financially than our parents.
—Many people think they would have **been better off** study**ing** English when they were children. But it's never too late.
—I hope the next generation will **be better off**. (Stress the word *off* here.)

√ ? **4. be cooped úp (in)**

Definition: be inside a place feeling like you have little freedom

Origin: This probably comes from the idea of a chicken coop, which is the enclosed area where chickens live.

S1: How was your vacation in the mountains?
S2: Not so great. There was a big storm, so we **were cooped up in** the cabin for most of the week.

—I need to get out of the house. I've **been cooped up** here for three days with a cold, and I need some fresh air.

√ ? **5. be at the énd of one's rópe**

Definition: be under a lot of stress, at the breaking point

Note: If you are *at the end of your rope,* you are at a point that is not very strong and is not balanced.

S1: I**'m at the end of my rope.** I can't take it anymore. There's too much pressure.

S2: Don't you think you need to see a doctor? It sounds like you need some help.

S1: What happened to her? I saw her run out of the office.

S2: She said she **was at the end of her rope,** and she quit.

S1: What was bothering her?

S2: She said that nothing ever changed around here except that she kept getting more and more work that she couldn't handle. She told us that she was going to take a long vacation, and then look for a new career.

√ ? 6. For crýing out lóud!

Definition: This is an exclamation of anger.

Origin: This is probably a euphemism for the exclamation "For Christ's sake!" People did not want to say that, and somehow for crying . . . came out as a substitute. (A euphemism is a special expression that is used to avoid saying something else. An example would be the expression *pass away*, which is often used instead of the word *die*.)

—**For crying out loud!** How many times do I have to ask you to turn out the lights?

—**For crying out loud!** Will you guys be quiet for a minute?

Another Expression with "cry": **It's nó úse crýing over spílt mílk (or Dón't crý over spílt mílk!)** = It's no use complaining about what is past; it cannot be changed.

S1: Oh no, why did I sell my guitar?
S2: I don't know. Can you get it back?
S1: No.
S2: Well, **it's no use crying over spilt milk.** (*or* **Don't cry over spilt milk.**) Save your money for a new one.

√ ? 7. lóse one's héad

Definition: go crazy; (sometimes) panic

S1: You bought that old car???
S2: I don't know why I did it. I guess I **lost my head**. At the time, it looked like a good deal.

S1: What did they do during the earthquake?
S2: Well, some people **lost their heads** and screamed and ran outside. But others went under doorways and tables and waited for the shaking to stop.

√ ? 8. knock oneself óut

Definition: try very hard, making oneself very tired

Stuck in an Elevator—Cooped Up and Sitting Tight

Grammar Note: This expression can be followed by an infinitive or a gerund.

—We **knocked ourselves out** to be here even though there's a big storm, but no one else is here.
—We **knocked ourselves out** driv**ing** in the storm, but no one else is here.

Contrast: **be knocked óut** = *be very tired*

—I'**m** too **knocked out** to go to the movies tonight. Sorry.
—He **was** so **knocked out** that he went straight to bed.

Contrast: **knock someone óut** = hit someone on the head and cause him or her to become unconscious. This is the literal meaning of the expression. It is used in boxing and in fights in general.

—That fighter is going to **knock** the other guy **out** right away.

√ ?   **9. máke dó**

Definition: manage with what one has, even though it isn't enough or perfect

S1: How are they these days?
S2: They're managing to **make do** on the little money they have. They're still looking for better jobs.

—This elevator isn't exactly comfortable, but we have no choice but to **make do.**
—There isn't much in the refrigerator, but we'll just have to **make do** with what we have until we can get to the store.

√ ?   **10. clímb the wálls**

Definition: go crazy, especially in an enclosed space or in a situation that is very boring

—I'd be **climbing the walls** if I lived in an apartment this small.
—I wonder if the rain will ever stop. The kids are **climbing the walls.**

Related Expression: **gét/háve cábin féver** = be in an enclosed space for a long time so you feel that you need to get out

—We've been cooped up so long because of the snow, I'm **getting cabin fever.**

—The kids **have cabin fever.** Let's take them out so they can run around for a while.

√ ? 11. kéep a lével héad

Definition: keep calm

S1: The fire was scary, but everyone **kept a level head** and no one panicked.

S2: That's lucky. It could've been a lot worse.

√ ? 12. sít tíght

Definition: stay in one place calmly and wait for something or someone

—**Sit tight** and I'll be right there. Don't go anywhere.

—**Sit tight.** Help is on the way.

—We need to **sit tight** and wait.

√ ? 13. dwéll on

Definition: think too much about something

—Let's not **dwell on** the dangerous things that can happen while we're stuck in this elevator. Let's talk about something else.

—It's not good to **dwell on** the past so much. Think about the future.

√ ? 14. come thróugh

Definition: survive a difficult situation

—I have good news for you. He **came through** the surgery beautifully. He'll be fine.

—They're lucky. Their town **came through** the war with little damage.

—They **came through** that time on the elevator as friends. In fact, they went out to a very special dinner after they were rescued.

Exercises

1. Mini-Dialogues

Below are two exercises with two columns each, A and B. Column A contains the first lines of dialogues, and column B contains possible responses. For each opening line in column A, choose the *best* response from column B. Sometimes more than one response is possible. Not all responses can be used.

When checking the exercise in class, perform each mini-dialogue. One student should read an item from column A, and another student should respond with the answer from column B.

1. A

____ 1. I'm at the end of my rope. I've been cooped up in this house for too long.

____ 2. Chris and Debra are coming over for dinner. Do we have enough food?

____ 3. Sit tight. Don't go anywhere. I'll be right back, OK?

____ 4. Don't dwell on the trouble you had. Tell me about the good parts of your trip.

____ 5. The plane trip was really bumpy. There was a lot of turbulence.

____ 6. Do you think people are worse off than they used to be?

1. B

a. I don't know where to begin.
b. Well, it looks like you came through it all right.
c. Please hurry. I don't want to be alone.
d. I don't know. We'll have to make do with what we have.
e. I saw them out of the corner of my eye.
f. You're not so sick anymore. Why don't you take a walk?
g. Not all, but some certainly are.

2. A

____ 1. For crying out loud! Where have you been?

____ 2. This is the last straw. It's happened too many times before.

____ 3. Don't you think we'd be better off living on an island?

____ 4. I'm totally shocked. Out of the blue they said they were leaving the country forever.

____ 5. Come on. Take a break. You've been knocking yourself out for hours.

____ 6. Quiet, everyone! This discussion is really getting out of hand.

2. B

a. Thanks. Maybe I'll take a few minutes.
b. I know. It's my fault. I promise I won't do it again.
c. Stuck in traffic. Sorry we're so late.
d. Well, it depends on which one.
e. I agree. Only one person will talk at a time. OK?
f. Did they give you any reasons?
g. I'm knocked out. I'm going to bed.

2. Choosing the Idiom

The following conversation is between a rescue worker and the two people who are stuck in the elevator. Fill in the blanks with the best possible expressions from the list. Pay special attention to how the expressions are used grammatically. You may need to consider verb tenses, subject-verb agreement, pronouns, active vs. passive voice, etc. Not all of the expressions in the list can be used. After you finish, practice reading the sentences aloud.

out of the blue   out of hand
cooped up   be at the end of one's rope
knock oneself out   come through
keep a level head   dwell on
climb the walls   be better off
sit tight

RESCUE WORKER: Hello in there! How're you doing?

MR. CLAUSTROPHOBIA: Could be better! Hey, I'm sure glad to see you.

MRS. CALM: So am I. What's your name?

Rescue Worker: I'm Bill, and my friends and I are working hard to locate the problem and get you out of this elevator.

MR. CLAUSTROPHOBIA: You mean we can't get out yet? I can't stand being

(1) _____ in here. I'm

starting to (2) _____ .

RESCUE WORKER: I know. Just (3) _____ for
another few minutes, and I'm sure we'll be able to get this thing moving again.

MR. CLAUSTROPHOBIA: But I (4) _____ . You've got to get me out of here!

MRS. CALM: Now, Mr. Claustrophobia, you'll be just fine. Try to relax. Bill will help us.

MR. CLAUSTROPHOBIA: You're right, Mrs. Calm. I'm sorry. You know, Bill, I'm lucky I got stuck in this elevator with Mrs. Calm because she's

been a big help. She's been (5) _____

_____ , trying to get me to calm down. All through

this she has (6) _____ . The
truth is that she's absolutely great. Mrs. Calm, will you have dinner with me tonight if we ever get out of this elevator?

MRS. CALM: Why, Mr. Claustrophobia, it would be a pleasure. See, I told you that we'd (7) _____ this just fine.

3. Dictation

Your teacher or one of your classmates will read the dictation for this lesson from Appendix A, or you will listen to the dictation on the audio program. You will hear the dictation three times. First, just listen. Second, as you listen, write the dictation on a separate piece of paper. Third, check what you have written.

4. Pronunciation Part 1—Contractions

Pronounce the contractions from the "Stuck in the Elevator" dialogue. (When a contraction has more than one syllable, the stressed syllable is in capital letters.)

Contractions	Pronunciation	
can't	kant	/kænt/
what's	wuts	/wʌts/
I'm	eyem	/aɪm/
wasn't	WUzint	/wʌ́-zɪnt/
don't	dont	/doʊnt/
they'll	thayl	/ðeɪl/
isn't	Izint	/í-zɪnt/
we'll	weeel	/wil/
you're	yor	/yɔr/
I'd	eyed	/aɪd/
Let's	lets	/lɛts/
you've	yoov	/yuv/
that'll	THAdul	/ðǽ-dəl/

Practice 1: Speak

Underline the contractions in the dialogue and then practice saying the dialogue aloud with a partner.

Pronunciation Part 2—Reduced Forms (Reductions)

As you know, many words that you have difficulty understanding in fast streams of speech are easily recognizable to you when they are written in their full forms. The reason for your difficulty in understanding is that native speakers often "reduce" the full forms when they speak. Take a look at this list of the full and reduced forms that appear in this lesson's dialogue. (When a reduced form has more than one syllable, the stressed syllable is in capital letters.)

Full Form	Pronunciation of Reduced Form	
out of	OWda	/aʊ dǿ/
going to	GONna or GOing ta	/gʌ́nə/ /góʊɪŋtə/
to	ta	/tə/

would have been	WUDuv been	/wʌ́dəvbɪn/
do you	da ya	/duyə/
don't know	doNO or duNO	/doʊnóʊ/
for	fer	/fər/
you	ya	/yə/
have to	HAFta	/hǽf.tə/
and	'n	/ən/
you're	yer	/yər/
or	er	/ər/
climbing	CLI-min'	/klǽɪ.mɪn/
don't you	DONcha	/dóʊn-tʃə/

Practice 2: Listen

Circle the full forms listed above in the dialogue. Then listen to the tape to see if you can hear how their reduced forms are pronounced. You do not need to be concerned about actually saying the reduced forms, but recognizing them when you hear them will help your comprehension.

Practice 3: Pronunciation Review

Review the rules for stress and intonation in Lessons 1 through 4. Then apply these rules to the conversation of the three people in Exercise 2 of this lesson. Circle or put accent marks on the words that should receive the most stress, and draw arrows to indicate where the intonation should go up or down. Then, in groups of three, perform the Exercise 2 conversation aloud.

5. Questions for Discussion and/or Writing

(For more detailed instructions, see Lesson 1, page 13.)

For Discussion: You can answer these questions orally in groups or in the *Walk and Talk* activity in Appendix B.

For Writing: You can write your own answers to these questions, or you can write the responses that you received from students during the *Walk and Talk* activity.

Questions

1. What are three to five events that can happen out of the blue and surprise people? Make a list.
2. Are people in your native country generally better off or worse off financially than they were twenty or thirty years ago? Explain.
3. When people don't have enough money to buy a lot of things, what are some things they do to "make do"?
4. Have you ever been cooped up in a car, train, bus, plane, or boat for a long trip? If yes, describe how you (and the others) felt and what you did to pass the time.
5. What are some kinds of work that you have knocked yourself out doing?

6. Write Your Own

Here are some situations along with expressions from this lesson. Use your imagination and write your own sentences or dialogues to describe, explain, or act out the situations. Try to use at least two of the expressions in parentheses.

1. You and some friends or family members have rented a cabin in the mountains in the winter. Unexpectedly, there's a blizzard (a big snowstorm), and you have to stay inside. You all sit in the living room and complain to one another. Write what you say. (*be cooped up, climb the walls, be better off, make do*)

   _____

   _____

   _____

   _____

   _____

2. You are very surprised to receive a letter from someone you went to school with many years ago. He or she tried very hard to find your address and finally got it from one of your relatives. You remember that the two of you had had an argument long ago, and are glad that this old friend wants to forget the past and get in touch with you again. You tell another friend about the letter. Write what you say. (*out of the blue, knock oneself out, It's no use crying over spilt milk, dwell on*)

   _____

   _____

   _____

   _____

   _____

3. There has been a problem of cheating on tests in a class. After the last test, the teacher warned the students that if anyone cheated again, everyone's test would be thrown away. Someone cheats again, and the teacher is very upset. Write what she or he says to the class. (*the last straw, out of the corner of one's eye, out of hand, be at the end of one's rope*)

   _____

   _____

   _____

   _____

   _____

Choose one of your corrected "Write Your Own" sections and dictate it to a partner or group or your entire class. Before you do this, think about the pronunciation points you have studied and mark your sentences.

7. Scene Three

Consider the opening conversation between Mr. Claustrophobia and Mrs. Calm to be the first scene of a play. And consider the conversation in Exercise 2 with the rescue worker, Bill, to be Scene Two. On your own, with a partner, or in a small group, now write Scene Three. Imagine that it is the same evening, and Mr. Claustrophobia and Mrs. Calm are having dinner at a very nice restaurant.

As you write, see if any of the expressions from this or other lessons fit into the conversation. Also, feel free to use other expressions that you know. But don't feel that it is necessary to have an idiom in every sentence.

If possible, groups of students can practice various versions of Scene Three and then perform them for the class. You might even want to videotape these scenes.

8. Chain Story

Here is the beginning of a story. Continue the story by going around the room and having each student orally add a sentence, or get into small groups and have group members each add a sentence one by one. Try to have three to five expressions in your story. It will be helpful if the expressions from the dialogue are written on the board for all to see.

This is the story of a wonderful old woman named Mrs. Calm. She had a magical way of appearing in emergency situations where people needed help. One day. . . .

9. Role Playing

Using the new expressions from this lesson, act out the following role play. The new expressions should be written on the board.

Two people are climbing the stairs to the 12th floor in order to avoid taking the elevator that gave Mr. Claustrophobia so much trouble. They talk about what happened to Mr. Claustrophobia and their own fear of being stuck in an elevator.

Possible starting line: I think we're better off taking the stairs than the elevator.

10. Tic Tac Toe

In this variation of tic tac toe, to get an X or an O you need to create a grammatically correct sentence that is logical in meaning. Here is a game to start you off. Create as many games as you like, using expressions from Lesson 6. And if you would like to review expressions from any other lesson that you have studied, add them to the game.

out of the blue	get out of hand	be better off
be cooped up	be knocked out	make do
climb the walls	sit tight	dwell on

11. Expand on What You Now Know

In this lesson, you studied two-word verbs with the words *knock* and *come*. Many more expressions exist in combination with these verbs.

You already know:

knock oneself out   **come** through

To learn some more expressions with these words, with a partner ask a native speaker to help you fill out this chart. In order to do this kind of assignment, see Appendix C, "Contact Assignments," for information on how to start a conversation with a native speaker of English.

Pronunciation Note: Remember to stress the second part of two-word verbs.

	Meaning	**Sample Sentence**
knock		
on	_____	_____
		_____
off	_____	_____
		_____

	it off	_____	_____
			_____
	over	_____	_____
			_____
come			_____
	about	_____	_____
			_____
	across	_____	_____
			_____
	off	_____	_____
			_____
	to	_____	_____
			_____

In this lesson you learned the expression *out of the blue.* There are some more very common expressions starting with *out of.* You may want to find out what they mean:

out of sight, out of mind
out of bounds
out of breath
out of date
out of line
out of luck
out of one's hands
out of the ordinary
out of the question
out of thin air

12. Connect Your Class to the Real World

Every week, on your own or with a partner, find three expressions from the real world that are new to you. Keep an inventory in your notebook or on 3 x 5 cards, following the format in Appendix D, "Student Idiom Collection." Be ready to share what you found in small groups or with your entire class.

Crossword Puzzle for Lessons 5 and 6

Across

1. He came ____ the surgery very well.
4. Please don't leave me ____ . I need to have company.
7. I'm not going to rule that ____ . It's still possible.
8. They didn't have much, but they ____ do with what they had.
10. I don't have a ____ about what he's talking about. Do you?

Down

1. I've got to hand it to ____ . They did a great job.
2. He knocked ____ out working on that assignment.
3. Who knows what's in ____ for us in the future.
4. She told me she's ____ the end of her rope.

11. She appeared at our house out of the
    ____.
13. Out of the corner of ____ eye I could
    see something moving.
14. Come on. That's unheard ____ .
16. For ____ out loud, what did you do that
    for?
18. We don't want to be cooped ____ in
    there for three days.
19. ____ me. I have no idea.
21. Yes, I'm sure beyond the ____ of a
    doubt.
22. Everything is still up in ____ air.
23. I don't have any idea. Your ____ is as
    good as mine.
26. I don't have the ____ idea where they
    went.
29. They need to take a walk. They have
    ____ fever.
30. He lost his book. All his work went down
    the ____ .

5. We'd be better ____ if we could start all
   over.
6. I didn't knock ____ out. In fact, I didn't
   do any work.
9. Listen, let's not ____ on what happened.
   Let's change the subject.
10. It's totally beyond my ____ how that
    could've happened.
12. It's over. It's ____ milk.
15. He had a sinking ____ that something
    terrible happened.
17. I'm ____ out. I need a nap.
18. It's no ____ crying over spilt milk. You
    can't change what happened.
20. Getting stuck in the elevator was the
    last ____ . He went nuts.
23. What's ____ into them? They're acting
    crazy.
24. It'll take some time for that news to ____
    in.
25. Sit ____ . I'll be there in a minute.
27. Don't panic. There is no point in your
    losing your ____ .
28. His heart ____ when he heard the news.

Technology Today— Grappling with Computers

Warm-Up

Ask a partner the following questions and then compile the responses of the entire class.

Question	Response
1. Do you use a computer?	
2. If yes, what kind do you use?	
3. If you have children, do they use computers?	
4. On a scale of 1–5 (with 5 being the most comfortable), how comfortable are you with computers?	

Dialogue Steps

Choose one or more of the following:
(a) Listen to the tape as you read the dialogue.
(b) Say the dialogue in pairs.
(c) Have two volunteers perform the dialogue in front of the class.

(Part 1)

MOM: Well, **there are no ifs, ands, or buts about it.** Anna **is** completely **at home with** all this technology.

DAD: Isn't it great? She doesn't have the fear of technology that so many of us have. It's amazing to think that her generation has grown up with VCRs, answering machines, cordless phones, computer games . . . They **take** all that stuff **for granted.**

MOM: That's for sure. To think there are kids her age who have never changed a TV channel without a remote control! Can you imagine?

DAD: I'm sure you're right. Hey—remember our old computer?

MOM: How could I forget it? I don't ever want to see that old dinosaur again.

DAD: Oh, come on.

MOM: Really. It made me so frustrated.

DAD: Well, it's true that new computers **are a quantum leap over** the old ones. But still, it's hard for me to **grapple with** learning programs even on the new computers.

MOM: I know what you mean. You know, I've been thinking that maybe we should take an evening class. What do you think? We could get a babysitter.

DAD: Wow . . . I'm really glad to hear you say that because I've thought a lot about taking a class, but I've always **dragged my feet.** I don't know why, really.

(Part 2) At home after the first computer class

MOM: Look at you! You're really **plugging away at** that computer!

DAD: Nothing could **tear me away.** You know, if it weren't for our class, I'd **be in a bind** right now trying to figure out what to do. But I'm doing OK. The class really helps.

MOM:	That's the truth. **I'll take** a teacher **over** an instruction manual **any day.** Hey—did I tell you that I want to get a modem? I want to **get online.** Don't you think we've **held off** long enough? I want to have e-mail.
DAD:	That teacher sure **won you over.** A few months ago you didn't even know what e-mail was!
MOM:	Well, I have to admit, this whole world of computers **is growing on me.**
DAD:	Sounds like you'**re apt to** go back to school and get some sort of degree in computers.
MOM:	You never know. . . .

Guess the Meanings

Below is a list of paraphrases of five of the idiomatic expressions contained in the dialogue. On your own or with a partner, try to guess the five.

Paraphrase	Idiomatic Expression from the Dialogue
1. There is no doubt.	_____
2. working hard at	_____
3. are much, much better than	_____
4. deal with	_____
5. pull/take me away	_____

■ Understanding the New Expressions

Figure It Out with Others and/or On Your Own

(For more detailed instructions, see Lesson 1, page 3.)

WITH OTHERS:

Work in small groups to go through this information. The leader of each group should make sure that everyone participates equally.

ON YOUR OWN:

Read this entire section carefully.

For each expression circle the check mark or question mark in the margin to indicate whether or not you understand the information given.

All Clear?

1. Thére are no ífs, ánds, or búts (about it).

Definition: There can be absolutely no questions or comments (about it). There is no doubt (about it).

Note: The *it* in this expression is often explained in the sentence that comes before or after.

S1: We need a vacation. **There are no ifs, ands, or buts about it.** (Or: **There are no ifs, ands, or buts, about it.** We need a vacation.)
S2: OK. I'm not arguing. Where do you want to go?

S1: No TV tonight. I want you to read your book and go to bed early.
S2: But, Mom, there's a great program on at 9!
S1: Listen, **there are no ifs, ands, or buts** . . . I don't want to discuss it.

2. be/féel at hóme (with or in)

Definition: be/feel comfortable with or in

—You**'re** really **at home with** that guitar. How long have you been playing?
—She**'s** very **at home with** people from different countries.
—They **feel** very much **at home with** each other.
—Look how he**'s** so **at home in** the water! He swims just like a fish.

3. táke something or someone for gránted/ táke it for gránted that . . .

Definition: habitually expect something or someone to do things or be a certain way, and not really show any special appreciation

S1: In California we **take good weather for granted.**
S2: But you have earthquakes there.
S1: True, but the weather's great.

S1: Why's he upset?
S2: He says his girlfriend **takes him for granted.** You know, she assumes that he'll always be the one to plan something nice for every Saturday night. He'd like her to make an effort sometimes, too.

—You know, we **take it for granted that** we will always have food on the table, but not everyone in the world can do that. I think we need to think about that.
—You **take it for granted that** I'm going to be the one to cook and clean all the time, but I have news for you. Those days are over now that I'm going back to work full-time.

4. a qúantum léap over something

Definition: much, much better than something else

Origin: This expression comes from the field of nuclear physics. According to the *Morris Dictionary of Word and Phrase Origins,* we use "a quantum leap" (or jump) to mean "any sudden and dramatic change, especially in the field of scientific research, scholarship and learning."

S1: TVs today are **a quantum leap over** the TVs we used to have.
S2: What do you mean?
S1: Well, for one thing, we didn't even have remote controls.
S2: Do you mean that you actually had to get up to change the channel?

—Education years ago was a **quantum leap over** education today.
—Many people find the quality of their lives today to be a **quantum leap over** the quality of their lives years ago.

√ ? 5. grápple with

Definition: deal with/struggle with something difficult or complicated

—The legislature **is grappling with** the new budget.
—The President **is grappling with** ways to cut the budget.
—**Grappling with** English is hard, but I'm trying.
—They're trying to **grapple with** the problems in their marriage by going to a marriage counselor.

√ ? 6. drág one's féet

Definition: be slow about doing something that is not particularly pleasant; procrastinate or delay

Note: to *drag* is to pull something on the floor or ground; perhaps it is too heavy to actually pick up

S1: You said you'd be all packed by 2 o'clock. What happened?
S2: I'm sorry. I've been **dragging my feet** all day.

S1: They promised to pay me yesterday, but they'**re dragging their feet.**
S2: They can't do that! You have to go in and talk to them.

Other Expressions with "drag":
drag something óut = make something last an unnecessarily long time

—She **dragged** the story **out** for a whole hour, giving us every little detail.
drag ón = continue on and on in a boring way
—The movie **dragged on** for five long hours.
(Use *out* when you actually have a human subject, such as in "She dragged the story out" or "He dragged the lecture out." Use *on* in sentences such as "The movie dragged on" or "The lecture dragged on.")

drag someone awáy from = take someone away from something he/she doesn't want to leave (the same as *tear someone away from*)

—It's hard to **drag him away from** the computer these days. He's addicted.
—Please **drag me away from** all these desserts. Otherwise, I might eat them.

Whát a drág! (See Lesson 3.)

√ ? 7. plug awáy at

Definition: continuously work very hard at something

S1: You've been really **plugging away at** tennis. I see a lot of improvement.
S2: Thanks. I try to practice every day.

S1: Where is she?
S2: She's **plugging away at** the computer. I think she has a paper due tomorrow.

√ ? 8. tear someone awáy from something

Definition: pull someone away from something that he/she doesn't want to leave (the same as *drag someone away from*)

S1: Can you **tear yourself away from** the TV long enough to have dinner?
S2: I don't think so. This is a big game. How about eating in front of the TV tonight?

S1: Excuse me, can I **tear you away** (from your friends or from a meeting) for a minute? I have to tell you something.
S2: Sure. I'll be right there.

√ ? 9. be in a bínd

Definition: be in a difficult situation

S1: I'**m** really **in a bind.** I don't know what to do. Can you give me some advice?
S2: I'll try. Tell me what the problem is.

√ ? 10. someone will táke X̀ over Ý́ ány dáy

Definition: someone prefers X to Y

—I'**ll take** rock music **over** classical **any day.**
—**They'll take** driving **over** flying **any day.**
—I'**ll take** a good restaurant **over** a fast-food place **any day.**

√ ? 11. gét/be onlíne

Definition: have a computer connected to a modem, which is connected to a telephone line so that it is possible to be on the Internet.

S1: Can I have your e-mail address?
S2: I wish I had one, but I**'m** not **online.**

—My office **is** finally **online,** so I can access the Internet. (*access* is computer language for "connect to.")

Other Computer-Related Vocabulary:

boot úp = what a computer does when it is first turned on; it basically gets itself ready to accept your commands
clíck on the móuse
dóuble clíck = click two times
drág the móuse = move the mouse without lifting it off the mouse pad
cýberspace = the mythical "place" or "space" where information travels from one computer to another

√ ? 12. hold óff

Definition: postpone something so that something else can happen first

Note: *Hold off* has a strong sense of the need to wait for something to happen first before something else takes place. For this reason, the word *until* is often used (or implied) with this expression.

Grammar Note: This expression is often followed by a gerund.

Hold off (wait)	**for something else to happen first**
Let's **hold off** gett**ing** a computer	until we are sure about what we want.
	until the prices come down.
	because we don't have the money right now.
We **held off** buy**ing** a car	until we saved enough money.
Hold off before you say anything.	You need to check your information first.

√ ? 13. win someone óver

Definition: get the support of someone, usually after he or she has resisted

—At first I wanted a computer just to be able to type. I didn't care about modems and things like that. Then one of my friends showed me what he can do online, and believe me, he **won me over** in ten minutes.
—That politician's speech was very, very powerful. You could see from people's faces that he was **winning them over** with his ideas.

√ ? **14. gró̇w on someone**

Definition: (something is) slowly liked by someone who didn't care much for it at first

S1: I thought you didn't like this kind of food.
S2: I didn't at first. But it's kind of **growing on me.** (I'm starting to like it.)

S1: Can I hear that again? I never thought I'd like that kind of music, but I have to admit, it's **growing on me.**

√ ? **15. be ápt to**

Definition: be likely to, be inclined to

S1: You'**re apt to** go deaf if you don't turn the music down!
S2: Come on. Don't exaggerate.

—During weather like this, people **are apt to** stay home a lot more.
—He's so sad these days, he'**s apt to** start crying at any moment.

Exercises

1. Mini-Dialogues

Below are two exercises with two columns each, A and B. Column A contains the first lines of dialogues, and column B contains possible responses. For each opening line in column A, choose the *best* response from column B. Sometimes more than one response is possible. Not all responses can be used.

When checking the exercise in class, perform each mini-dialogue. One student should read an item from column A, and another student should respond with the answer from column B.

1. A

__e__ **1.** I was surprised to see you on the bus today.

__g__ **2.** I love skiing. I'll take winter over summer any day.

__a__ **3.** We've been grappling with this math problem for an hour, and we still can't find the answer!

__d__ **4.** There are no ifs, ands, or buts. This is what we're going to do.

__c__ **5.** They held off having children until they were in their thirties.

__b__ **6.** This house is a quantum leap over the last one we lived in.

1. B

a. Maybe the teacher can help us.

b. That's for sure!

c. That's a long time to wait, isn't it?

d. That's not fair!

e. Yeah, my car broke down. Now I see how much I take it for granted.

f. Don't drag your feet.

g. That's pretty unusual. I think most people would say the opposite.

2. A

__d__ **1.** At first I didn't believe him, but then he won me over.

__b__ **2.** When are you going to take a break? You've been plugging away at that all day!

__g__ **3.** You know, I was really in a bind, and you helped me a lot. And I know you were very busy. Thank you.

__a__ **4.** Can I tear you away from that book? I have to ask you something.

__f__ **5.** I can see that you're really at home on ice skates.

__c__ **6.** The ceremony dragged on for over an hour!

2. B

a. Sure. What is it?

b. If I stop now, I'll lose my concentration.

c. Was anyone snoring?

d. How? What did he say?

e. He's apt to be a big help.

f. Uh-huh. I started when I was three.

g. Well, that's what friends are for.

2. Choosing the Idiom

The following is a conversation called a "chat" that is taking place online between two strangers from different countries. Fill in the blanks with the best possible expressions from the list. Pay special attention to how the expressions are used grammatically. You may need to consider verb tenses, subject-verb agreement, pronouns, active vs. passive voice, etc. Not all of the expressions in the list can be used. After you finish, practice reading the sentences aloud.

tear someone away	a quantum leap
grapple with	drag one's feet
be online	plug away
hold off	win __ over
be apt to	at home
will take	be in a bind

MARIO: What should we talk about today?

CATHY: I wanted to ask you if a lot of people (1) _____
_____ in your country.

MARIO: That's a good question. I don't know how many, but it's (2) _____
_____ over what it was ten years ago. How about in
the U.S.?

CATHY: The same. At first, many people (3) _____
getting home computers because they were so expensive, but now
that computers have gone down in price, they're everywhere. My

son is so (4) _____ at our computer that I

can't (5) _____ from it. And he

(6) _____ the computer over TV any day.

MARIO: What does he do? Play computer games?

CATHY: Yes, he does that, but he also does a lot of his homework on the

computer. He used to complain and (7) _____

_____ because he didn't want to do his homework, but that's
not true anymore. Now it's easier for him to write on the computer.

MARIO: Maybe because it's easy to make corrections and rewrite.

CATHY: Probably. You know, at first when he was (8) _____

_____ the keyboard, he didn't really like the computer. (:-(But he

(9) _____ at it, and now he loves it. (:-) In
fact, he asked for a computer of his own for his birthday.*

MARIO: Are you going to give him one?

CATHY: He tried to (10) _____ with a lot of
reasons why he should have one, but we finally said no. One
computer is enough for this family. They're still really expensive.

MARIO: It's the same here. But I bet in another twenty years, it'll be common
for kids to have their own. Listen, I'm sorry, but I have to go now. Do you
want to chat again tomorrow at the same time?

CATHY: Sure. Talk to you then. Bye.

---

*Note about (:-(and (:-): These are called "Smileys," and you can draw them with your keyboard. Turn this page
to the side to see the two facial expressions that are drawn. Some people who communicate a lot through
e-mail use Smileys to show how they feel. There are many Smileys. Check a library or bookstore for a book
with a collection of Smileys.

3. Dictation

Your teacher or one of your classmates will read the dictation for this lesson from Appendix A, or you will listen to the dictation on the audio program. You will hear the dictation three times. First, just listen. Second, as you listen, write the dictation on a separate piece of paper. Third, check what you have written.

4. Pronunciation—Voiced and Voiceless Consonants and the -*s* Ending

The final *s* is used to indicate:

● regular noun plurals (computer**s**)

● the third person singular form of verbs (want**s**)

● possessives (Mom'**s**)

These *s* endings can have three sounds: the voiceless /s/, the voiced /z/, or a new syllable, /ɪz/.

To determine which sound to use, you need to know whether the last sound (not letter) of a word is voiced or voiceless. All vowel sounds are voiced.

You can feel whether consonant sounds are voiced or voiceless by holding your hand against your throat and saying the sounds. If you feel a vibration, the sound is voiced.

Don't feel that it is necessary to memorize the chart below. It is for your reference. The best strategy for you when working on your pronunciation is to listen very carefully to the speech of native speakers. (For practice with troublesome consonant sounds, see Lesson 9.)

CONSONANTS

Letters	Sounds	Voiced	Voiceless	Example
b	/b/	x		**b**ut
c	/k/, /s/		x	**c**omputer, scien**c**e
d	/d/	x		**d**inosaur
f	/f/		x	**f**orget
g	/g/, /dʒ/	x		for**g**et, technolo**g**y
h	/h/		x	**h**ome
j	/dʒ/	x		**j**udge
k	/k/		x	thin**k**
l	/l/	x		mai**l**
m	/m/	x		progra**m**
n	/n/	x		wo**n**
p	/p/		x	com**p**uter
q	/kw/		x	**q**uite
r	/r/	x		**r**eally
s	/s/, /z/, /ʒ/	x	x	u**s**, i**s**, u**s**ual
t	/t/		x	grea**t**
v	/v/	x		**v**ery
w	/w/	x		**w**on
x	/ks/		x	si**x**

y	/y/	x	**y**ou
z	/z/	x	**z**oo
ch	/tʃ/, /ʃ/, /k/		x	**ch**ange, ma**ch**ine, te**ch**nology
sh	/ʃ/		x	**sh**e
th	/ð/, /θ/	x	x	**th**is, **th**ink
ng	/ŋ/	x		thi**ng**

Final -s Ending Rules				
Final Sound of Word	**Pronunciation of -s Ending**	**New Syllable Added?**	**Examples**	
voiceless	/s/	no	*asks* sounds like	/æsks/
voiced	/z/	no	*teachers* sounds like	/tí-tʃərz/
s, z, sh, ch, j	/ɪz/	yes	*classes* sounds like	/klǽ-sɪz/

Note: The answers for Practice 1, 2, and 3 can be found in Appendix E.

Practice 1

Here is a list of some of the regular nouns from this lesson's dialogue. With a partner, say both the singular and plural forms, and for the plural, circle which final sound should be used.

Singular	Plural	Final Sound		
1. home	homes	s	z	ɪz
2. fear	fears	s	z	ɪz
3. generation	generations	s	z	ɪz
4. VCR	VCRs	s	z	ɪz
5. machine	machines	s	z	ɪz
6. phone	phones	s	z	ɪz
7. game	games	s	z	ɪz
8. kid	kids	s	z	ɪz
9. channel	channels	s	z	ɪz
10. computer	computers	s	z	ɪz
11. leap	leaps	s	z	ɪz
12. one	ones	s	z	ɪz
13. class	classes	s	z	ɪz
14. thing	things	s	z	ɪz
15. month	months	s	z	ɪz
16. world	worlds	s	z	ɪz

17. In the expression "There are no <u>ifs</u>, <u>ands</u>, or <u>buts</u>," the underlined words are treated as nouns. How do you think you should pronounce the ends of these words? After you figure this out, practice saying the whole expression.

ifs	s	z	ɪz
ands	s	z	ɪz
buts	s	z	ɪz

Practice 2

Here are some of the verbs from the dialogue. Change them into the third person singular form and decide on how to pronounce the final *s*.

Verb	Third Person Singular	Final Sound
1. think	_____	S Z IZ
2. grow	_____	S Z IZ
3. take	_____	S Z IZ
4. change	_____	S Z IZ
5. imagine	_____	S Z IZ
6. remember	_____	S Z IZ
7. forget	_____	S Z IZ
8. want	_____	S Z IZ
9. see	_____	S Z IZ
10. know	_____	S Z IZ
11. get	_____	S Z IZ
12. hear	_____	S Z IZ
13. drag	_____	S Z IZ
14. explain	_____	S Z IZ
15. go	_____	S Z IZ

Practice 3

Read the following silently. As you read, write above the underlined words how you will pronounce the -s endings—as /s/, /z/ or /ɪz/. Then look at the words that follow these sounds. If any of these words start with a vowel sound, write linking lines between the *s* and the vowel sound that follows. (See Lesson 5 on linking.)

After you have finished marking these paragraphs, take turns reading them aloud with a partner.

Example: There are no ifs⏝ands⏝or buts⏝about it.

   Two <u>parents</u> are talking to each other about their young <u>daughter's</u> ability

to use a computer. The father <u>points</u> out that she isn't afraid of technology

because she has grown up with <u>VCRs</u>, answering <u>machines</u>, cordless <u>phones</u>,

and computer <u>games</u>. The mother <u>suggests</u> that they get a babysitter and

start computer <u>classes</u>.

After they start their <u>classes</u>, they use their computer more. In fact, the father <u>plugs</u> away at the computer every day. He's happy to have a teacher who <u>explains</u> <u>things</u> to him. His wife <u>agrees</u> because she doesn't like to read computer <u>manuals</u>. She is so enthusiastic about using a computer that she <u>wants</u> to buy a modem so they can get online. It <u>sounds</u> like everyone in this family <u>knows</u> more about <u>computers</u> every day.

Practice 4

Go through the dialogue in this lesson and any other lessons that you have studied. Find five plural nouns and five third person singular verbs, and complete the chart below. After you have completed the chart, practice saying the plural nouns and third person singular verbs and the words that come after them. Link these words when necessary.

-s Ending Word	Pronunciation of -s Ending			Word That Follows	Linked?		From Chapter #
1. _____	s	z	ɪz	_____	yes	no	_____
2. _____	s	z	ɪz	_____	yes	no	_____
3. _____	s	z	ɪz	_____	yes	no	_____
4. _____	s	z	ɪz	_____	yes	no	_____
5. _____	s	z	ɪz	_____	yes	no	_____
6. _____	s	z	ɪz	_____	yes	no	_____
7. _____	s	z	ɪz	_____	yes	no	_____
8. _____	s	z	ɪz	_____	yes	no	_____
9. _____	s	z	ɪz	_____	yes	no	_____
10. _____	s	z	ɪz	_____	yes	no	_____

Practice 5: Listen and Speak

Listen again to the dialogue, paying special attention to the pronunciation of the *s* endings. If possible, record yourself saying the dialogue and then analyze your pronunciation of these endings.

Practice 6: Pronunciation Review

Review the rules for thought groups and linking in Lesson 5. Then apply these rules to the conversation between Mario and Cathy in Exercise 2 of this lesson. Put parentheses around thought groups, and draw linking lines between words.

Also, circle all the contractions. Then perform the Exercise 2 dialogue aloud with a partner.

5. Questions for Discussion and/or Writing

(For more detailed instructions, see Lesson 1, page 13.)

For Discussion: You can answer these questions orally in groups or in the *Walk and Talk* activity in Appendix B.

For Writing: You can write your own answers to these questions, or you can write the responses that you received from students during the *Walk and Talk* activity.

Questions

1. What are some things that you took for granted when you were a child?
2. Because of progress in technology, many medical procedures have taken a quantum leap over what they were years ago. List two or three medical techniques that were unheard of twenty years ago.
3. What do you have to grapple with the most as you study English: grammar, writing, reading, listening, speaking, pronunciation, general vocabulary or idioms? Why? And which is the easiest for you?
4. There are some things that none of us like to do at home or at work. When do you drag your feet because you don't want to do something?
5. What do you prefer? Complete the following:

   I'd take _____ over _____ any day.

   I'd take _____ over _____ any day.

   I'd take _____ over _____ any day.

6. What is something that you'd like to do now, but you are holding off for a while? Why are you waiting?
7. Explain ways politicians try to win people over with their speeches.
8. What are you apt to be doing in ten years?

6. Write Your Own

Here are some situations along with expressions from this lesson. Use your imagination and write your own sentences or dialogues to describe, explain, or act out the situations. Try to use at least two of the expressions in parentheses.

1. A student talks about why she is saving money to buy a computer. She says she has waited too long to buy one and that she needs a computer for two reasons: to do research and to type her papers. She explains how much better computers are than typewriters. Write what she says. *(There are no ifs, ands, or buts about it, drag one's feet, be online, a quantum leap over)*

   _____

   _____

   _____

   _____

   _____

2. A mother complains to a friend about how her teenage children expect her to do everything for them. She shops, cooks, cleans, drives, and helps them with their problems. She believes that they spend too much time with their friends, and she wants them to do more around the house. Write what she says. *(take it for granted that, grapple with, tear someone away from)*

_____

_____

_____

_____

_____

3. A child tries to convince her father to let her keep a puppy that she got in front of a supermarket. He wants her to wait and get a cat, which is easier to take care of. She tries to convince him that he'll eventually love the dog and that she prefers dogs to cats. The father thinks the dog will be trouble, but he finally agrees to let his daughter have the dog. Write the conversation between the child and father. *(hold off, grow on someone, take X over Y any day, be apt to, win someone over)*

Child: _____

Father: _____

_____

_____

_____

Choose one of your corrected "Write Your Own" sections and dictate it to a partner or group or your entire class. Before you do this, think about the pronunciation points you have studied and mark your sentences.

7. Scene Two

Consider the opening conversation between Mom and Dad to be the first scene of a play. On your own, with a partner, or in a small group, now write Scene Two. Imagine that it is ten years later, and the girl, Anna, is getting ready to go to college. She is trying to convince her parents to buy her a computer.

As you write, see if any of the expressions from this or other lessons fit into the conversation. Also, feel free to use other expressions that you know. But don't feel that it is necessary to have an idiom in every sentence.

If possible, groups of students can practice various versions of Scene Two and then perform them for the class. You might even want to videotape these scenes.

8. Chain Story

Here is the beginning of a story. Continue the story by going around the room and having each student orally add a sentence, or get into small groups and have group members each add a sentence one by one. Try to have three to five expressions in your story. It will be helpful if the expressions from the dialogue are written on the board for all to see.

A retired couple decided that they needed to do something new and special. They realized that they had lots of free time, and wanted to learn about computers and the Internet. One Saturday, they walked into a computer store and. . . .

9. Role Playing

Using the new expressions from this lesson, act out the following role play. The new expressions should be written on the board.

Mom and Dad from the opening dialogue have invited Mom's parents over for dinner. They tell them about their progress with computers and are surprised to find out that they use computers all the time and are very comfortable with them.

Possible starting lines: Did we tell you that we've been taking a computer class? We're much more at home with our computer now than we used to be.

10. Tic Tac Toe

In this variation of tic tac toe, to get an X or an O you need to create a grammatically correct sentence that is logical in meaning. Here is a game to start you off. Create as many games as you like, using expressions from Lesson 7. And if you would like to review expressions from any other lesson that you have studied, add them to the game.

there are no
if's, ands
or buts
about it

be at
home with

grapple
with

drag
out

plug
away

be in a
bind

take x over
y any day

hold
off

be
apt to

11. Expand on What You Now Know

In this lesson, you studied two-word verbs with the words *drag, plug, tear, hold, win,* and *grow.* Many more expressions exist in combination with these words.

You already know:

drag out/on/away
tear away from
win someone over

plug away at
hold off
grow on

To learn some more expressions with these words, with a partner ask a native speaker to help you fill out this chart. In order to do this kind of assignment, see Appendix C, "Contact Assignments," for information on how to start a conversation with a native speaker of English.

Pronunciation Note: Remember to stress the second part of two-word verbs.

	Meaning	**Sample Sentence**
drag		
in/into	_____	_____
		_____
plug		
in/into	_____	_____
		_____
up	_____	_____
		_____

tear

    apart   _____   _____

                                                 _____

    down   _____   _____

                                                 _____

    off   _____   _____

                                                 _____

    up   _____   _____

                                                 _____

hold

    something
against someone   _____   _____

                                                 _____

    back   _____   _____

                                                 _____

    down   _____   _____

                                                 _____

    on   _____   _____

win

    at   _____   _____

                                                 _____

    back   _____   _____

                                                 _____

grow

    apart   _____   _____

                                                 _____

    into   _____   _____

                                                 _____

    out of   _____   _____

                                                 _____

12. Connect Your Class to the Real World

Every week, on your own or with a partner, find three expressions from the real world that are new to you. Keep an inventory in your notebook or on 3 x 5 cards, following the format in Appendix D, "Student Idiom Collection." Be ready to share what you found in small groups or with your entire class.

Violence in the Media— A Bone of Contention

Warm-Up

The subject of violence on TV, in movies, and in video games has been written about a great deal. Many people claim that the violence shown may not be necessary for a story, but it is included just for excitement and entertainment. This kind of "unnecessary" violence is called *gratuitous violence*.

Read the following quotations from newspaper reporters and then indicate whether you agree or not:

	Agree	Disagree	Not Sure
1. Is there too much violent entertainment on TV? Absolutely. Is all violent entertainment on TV bad? Absolutely not.—Greg Dawson, *Orlando Sentinel*	_____	_____	_____
2. It's human nature to seek easy answers to complex questions. Rather than acknowledge the root causes of violence as being deep and complicated, there's a tendency on the part			

	Agree	Disagree	Not Sure

of many to automatically blame television.—Howard Rosenberg, *Los Angeles Times*   _____   _____   _____

3. No one rational would argue against getting rid of gratuitous television violence. Obnoxious murders, knifings, beatings, you name it. They're everywhere, ranging across all of television, at the very least creating a feeling of unreasonable fear that affects the way we live our lives.—Howard Rosenberg, *Los Angeles Times*   _____   _____   _____

Discuss whether you think there is too much gratuitous violence in today's TV programs, movies, and video games, and whether it affects people's behavior. You can refer to the above quotations and, if possible, give specific examples of what you have seen.

Dialogue Steps

Choose one or more of the following:
(a)   Listen to the tape as you read the dialogue.
(b)   Say the dialogue in pairs.
(c)   Have two volunteers perform the dialogue in front of the class.

FRIEND 1   So, what do you think?

FRIEND 2:   Well, **it's nothing to write home about.**

FRIEND 1:   You must be kidding!

FRIEND 2:   Why do you say that?

FRIEND 1:   I think it's the best movie I've seen in years!

FRIEND 2:   With all that violence?

FRIEND 1:   It wasn't so violent.

FRIEND 2:   It certainly was. There was blood in practically every scene. And sometimes the violence **had no bearing on** the story. It was just put in for audiences who like to see blood. I don't know how they can **get away with** showing so much detail . . .

FRIEND 1:   Well, **from my standpoint,** there was a real anti-violence message in the movie. They showed how all that violence ended up in tragedy.

FRIEND 2:   But that's no excuse for being so graphic! Why did they have to show all that suffering? You know, **it's not written in stone that** audiences today need all that action to stay awake.

FRIEND 1: Those scenes weren't used to keep people awake. They were important parts of the story.

FRIEND 2: Sorry, but that argument just **doesn't hold water.** You could cut some of those scenes out and still have your story. And **as far as** sending an anti-violence message, they can do that without making an audience sick.

FRIEND 1: Now you're really **blowing** this whole thing **out of proportion.**

FRIEND 2: Am I? Look at the crime statistics. **It's a foregone conclusion that** violent TV programs and movies affect the way children behave. It's time for Hollywood to **be held accountable for** what it has caused.

FRIEND 1: Hollywood hasn't caused violence. And I **have yet to** hear of a child who committed a crime because of something he or she saw in the movies or on TV.

FRIEND 2: You haven't heard, but there are cases. Recently I heard about a 17-year-old accused of murdering his 13-year-old girlfriend's mother and brother after watching a movie on TV that was about a guy who killed his girlfriend's family.

FRIEND 1: Listen, you know this subject is **a bone of contention** between us. We've had heated arguments about this kind of thing before.

FRIEND 2: I know, but I don't want to ignore it. And I hope that someday I **get through to** you.

FRIEND 1: All I know is I **got my money's worth** tonight.

FRIEND 2: Well, I'll agree that the story was engrossing, but all that gory violence **drives me up the wall.**

FRIEND 1: Look, now we're back where we started. Let's just agree to disagree and go get a cup of coffee.

Guess the Meanings

Below is a list of paraphrases of five of the idiomatic expressions contained in the dialogue. On your own or with a partner, try to guess the five.

Paraphrase	Idiomatic Expression from the Dialogue
1. it's nothing special	_____
2. be made responsible for	_____
3. a matter of disagreement	_____
4. had nothing to do with	_____
5. exaggerating	_____

■ Understanding the New Expressions

Figure It Out with Others and/or On Your Own

(For more detailed instructions, see Lesson 1, page 3.)

WITH OTHERS:

Work in small groups to go through this information. The leader of each group should make sure that everyone participates equally.

ON YOUR OWN:

Read this entire section carefully.

For each expression, circle the check mark or question mark in the margin to indicate whether or not you understand the information given.

All Clear?

√ ?

1. (It's) nóthing to wríte hóme about

Definition: It's nothing special.

Pronunciation Note: The word *home,* the last stressed word in this expression, should receive the highest intonation.

S1: I heard you ate at the new restaurant on the corner. How was it?
S2: The food's **nothing to write home about,** but the atmosphere is nice.

Similar Expression: **léave a lót to be desíred** = not be adequate or satisfactory; not be as good as one would like.

S1: How was the movie?
S2: It **left a lot to be desired.** It was pretty boring.

√ ?

2. háve nó béaring on something

Definition: have no connection to

S1: The defense wanted to call her as a witness, but the judge wouldn't allow it. He said that her information **had no bearing on** the case.
S2: So she didn't testify?
S1: No, she didn't.

S1: Why did you say that? It **has no bearing on** what we're talking about.
S2: Yes, it does. Let me explain.

Contrast: **lóse one's béarings** = become lost, lose one's sense of direction

S1: Please don't let my grandmother go out alone. She always **loses her bearings.**
S2: Don't worry. I'll be with her every minute.

—Which way is west? I've **lost my bearings.**

√ ? **3. get awáy with something**

Definition: succeed in doing something undesirable or illegal without being caught or punished

Grammar Note: When you want to use a verb after this expression, turn it into a gerund.

S1: Those kids always **get away with** do**ing** whatever they want.
S2: That's because their parents don't set any limits.

S1: I wonder if I'll **get away with** turn**ing** in my friend's paper from two years ago. Do you think the teacher will remember it?
S2: Who knows? Is it worth it to you? Wouldn't you feel at all guilty?

Contrast: **get awáy with múrder** = do something very bad and not be caught or punished. This is a general expression—it doesn't specifically state what someone is getting away with.

S1: Do you see what those kids are doing? They're practically destroying the house!
S2: That's nothing new. Their parents always let them **get away with murder.**

√ ? **4. from ＿＿ 's stándpoint**

Definition: from ＿＿ 's point of view; in ＿＿ 's opinion

S1: Your position is very clear. But **from my standpoint,** you have come to the wrong conclusion because you haven't got all the necessary information.
S2: What information is that?

—**From my standpoint,** they shouldn't send soldiers over there. But **from his standpoint,** soldiers should be sent immediately. What do you think?

√ ? **5. It's nót wrítten in stóne (that)**

Definition: It's a situation that can be changed; how it is now does not have to be permanent. Even though something is traditional, not everyone will follow the tradition.

S1: My parents want me to study English, but I don't want to.

S2: You can study a different language. **It's not written in stone that** it has to be English.

S1: Why are your parents so upset?

S2: I told them that **it's not written in stone** that I'm going to get married someday. They were shocked. It wasn't what they expected to hear.

√ ? 6. something dóesn't hóld wáter

Definition: something (an explanation, a belief, etc.) is not strong and would not be able to be supported

S1: The suspect's alibi that he was at home at the time of the murder **doesn't hold water.**

S2: Why not?

S1: Because the police found out from the neighbors that he left home at 9:30 and didn't get back till after 11.

S1: I'm sorry, but your argument that TV doesn't affect kids' behavior **doesn't hold water.**

S2: How do you know?

S1: Don't you remember the story about the little boy who jumped off a building, thinking he could fly like Superman?

√ ? 7. as fár as

Definition: in regard to, related to

S1: **As far as** buy**ing** you a new car, I'm sorry, but the answer is no.

S2: Why did you change your mind?

S1: Because we decided that it's time for you to save money to buy one yourself.

Common Expressions with "as far as":
As fár as I knów, = What I know is that . . .

S1: Where are they?
S2: **As far as I know,** they went on vacation.

As fár as Í'm concérned, = In my opinion, . . .

S1: How did you like the movie?
S2: **As far as I'm concerned,** it was a big disappointment.

√ ? 8. blów something óut of propórtion

Definition: exaggerate the importance of something

S1: Why is your sister so upset with you?
S2: Because I told her that her outfit didn't look good on her, and she **blew what I said out of proportion.** She said that I'm always criticizing her. And all I was talking about was what she was wearing today.

S1: OK, I'll start the whole project over again.
S2: Wait a minute. Don't **blow this out of proportion.** I didn't say that you needed to redo the whole thing. I just said that you need to work more on one part of it.

√ ? 9. It's a fóregone conclúsion (that)

Definition: It's a result that cannot be avoided; the result was decided before.

Note: Fore is a prefix that means "before." Think of a weather *forecast* on TV or on the radio. The forecaster predicts what the weather will be in the future.

S1: You know, they have arranged marriages in their families.
S2: Really?
S1: Uh-huh. Since they were born, **it's been a foregone conclusion** that they were going to marry each other.
S2: I hope they like each other.

S1: There's no hope for me.
S2: Why not?
S1: **It's a foregone conclusion that** she'll be the winner.

√ ? 10. be héld accóuntable (for something)

Definition: be made responsible (for something)

S1: If they are the ones who made the mistake at the bank, then they should **be held accountable.**
S2: Do you think they should be fired?

S1: There's a lot of pollution in that river, and the nearby factory **is being held accountable for** it.
S2: So they'll have to pay for the clean-up, right?
S1: Uh-huh.

√ ? 11. **have yét to**

Definition: have not yet done something that was expected

Grammar Note: This expression is followed by the simple form of a verb to create an infinitive.

—They've been living together for two years, but they **have yet to** get married.
—I wrote to him three months ago, but I **have yet to** hear from him.
—She said she'd have all the work done by the end of the summer, but we **have yet to** hear from her.

√ ? 12. **a bóne of conténtion (between)**

Definition: something to argue or fight about

Origin: A bone of contention would literally be a bone that two dogs would fight over.

S1: When we're with them, don't bring up the subject of prayer in public schools.
S2: Why not?
S1: You know we disagree on that. It's **a bone of contention between** us, and I want to avoid it.

—Let's not talk about politics. You know it's a big **bone of contention between** us, and I don't feel like getting into a debate.

√ ? 13. **get thróugh to someone**

Definition: reach someone with ideas

S1: How can I **get through to** you? Why won't you believe me?
S2: It's not that I don't believe you. It's just that I don't agree with you.

S1: Did you get him to change his mind about dropping out of school?
S2: I tried, but I couldn't **get through to** him.

Contrast another meaning of "get through to:"

S1: Have you reached them yet?
S2: No. All the circuits are busy, and I can't **get through to** them.
S1: You can call them tomorrow.

√ ? **14. gét one's móney's wórth**

Definition: get the value of what one has paid for

S1: It was expensive, but we **got our money's worth.**
S2: What do you mean?
S1: We had a great time.

S1: The food here isn't very good, is it?
S2: No, and it's expensive. We're **not getting our money's worth,** are we?

√ ? **15. dríve someone up the wáll**

Definition: cause someone to feel angry, uncomfortable, or crazy

Idiomatic Synonyms: **dríve someone crázy, dríve someone núts**

S1: Have you read his new book?
S2: No. His ideas **drive me up the wall.**

—Can you change the station? That music **drives me up the wall.**

Exercises

1. Mini-Dialogues

Below are two exercises with two columns each, A and B. Column A contains the first lines of dialogues, and column B contains possible responses. For each opening line in column A, choose the *best* response from column B. Sometimes more than one response is possible. Not all responses can be used.

When checking the exercise in class, perform each mini-dialogue. One student should read an item from column A, and another student should respond with the answer from column B.

1. A

____ 1. I lost my job, and my life is over.
____ 2. Money has no bearing on my decision. I just don't want to go.
____ 3. Whoever threw a ball through that window will be held accountable.
____ 4. It's not written in stone that I have to go to college.
____ 5. The sound of chalk scratching on a blackboard drives me up the wall.

1. B

a. Come on. You have to give me a reason why.
b. How are you going to find out who did it?
c. I can't believe you're saying this. We've always expected you to go!
d. Don't say that. You're blowing it out of proportion.
e. I know what you mean.
f. It was nothing to write home about.

2. A

____ 1. A lot of people get away with stealing cars.
____ 2. When the old man lost his bearings, someone helped him out.
____ 3. In his family, the subject of politics is a bone of contention, so they try to avoid it.
____ 4. It sounds like you really got your money's worth out of that course.
____ 5 As far as going back there again, I don't know.
____ 6. She makes a lot of promises to the kids, but I have yet to see her keep them.

2. B

a. It's a foregone conclusion that they're doing it for the money.
b. There's no doubt about it. I learned a lot, and it helped me get a better job.
c. That's terrible. Don't they remind her?
d. That doesn't happen often enough. We need more people like that.
e. Oh, really? We like to have heated arguments around the dinner table.
f. How come? Don't the police look for them?
g. Why? What happened? Did you have a bad experience there the last time we went?

2. Choosing the Idiom

The following is a poem about an elderly man's love of computers. *It will help you when you fill in the blanks to look at the last word of the following line. The answer will often rhyme with that word.* Pay special attention to how the expressions are used grammatically. You may need to consider verb tenses, subject-verb agreement, pronouns, active vs. passive voice, etc. Not all of the expressions in the list can be used. After you finish, practice reading the sentences aloud.

get through to
from my standpoint
as far as
a bone of contention
doesn't hold water
nothing to write home about

have yet to
blow ____ out of proportion
leave a lot to be desired
have no bearing on
drive ____ up the wall
It's not written in stone

This may be (1) _____ ,
but I think computers are a great invention.

My old typewriter (2) _____ .
But now when I work I can do anything at all.

Some people say computers are (3) _____.
But (4) _____ , they are great—without any doubt!

(5) _____ that everyone needs to learn how to
use a computer.
But any argument that computers aren't important just

(6)_____ .

I (7) _____ hear of a child who doesn't like computer games.
And many adults apparently feel the same.

I hope you won't take what I say lightly.
You may soon find yourself at a computer nightly.

How can I (8) _____ those of you

Who believe I'm (9) _____ the value of a computer _____ ?

Just come over to my house,
Pick up my mouse,
And enter the world of computer devotion.

3. Dictation

Your teacher or one of your classmates will read the dictation for this lesson
from Appendix A, or you will listen to the dictation on the audio program. You
will hear the dictation three times. First, just listen. Second, as you listen, write the
dictation on a separate piece of paper. Third, check what you have written.

4. Pronunciation—Voiced and Voiceless Consonants and the -*ed* Ending

The final *ed* that is used to form the past tense of regular verbs can have
three sounds: the voiceless /*t*/, the voiced /*d*/ or a new syllable, ɪd.

To determine which sound to use, you need to know whether the last sound (not letter) is voiced or voiceless. All vowels are voiced.

To find out whether particular consonant sounds are voiced or voiceless, look at the consonant chart in Lesson 7 on page 126.

Past Tense Ending Rules				
Final Sound of Regular Verb	Pronunciation of -ed Ending	New Syllable Added?	Examples	
voiceless	/t/	no	*looked* sounds like	/lʊkt/
voiced	/d/	no	*caused* sounds like	/kɔzd/
t or d	/ɪd/	yes	*needed* sounds like	/ní-dɪd/

Note: The answers for Practice 1 and 2 can be found in Appendix E.

Practice 1

Here is a list of some of the regular verbs from this lesson's dialogue. They have been put into the past tense. Decide on how the -ed endings should be pronounced, and then practice saying these verbs with a partner.

Past Tense Verb **Final Sound**

1. liked   t   d   ɪd
2. showed   t   d   ɪd
3. ended   t   d   ɪd
4. needed   t   d   ɪd
5. stayed   t   d   ɪd
6. used   t   d   ɪd
7. looked   t   d   ɪd
8. affected   t   d   ɪd
9. behaved   t   d   ɪd
10. caused   t   d   ɪd
11. committed   t   d   ɪd
12. listened   t   d   ɪd
13. wanted   t   d   ɪd
14. hoped   t   d   ɪd
15. agreed   t   d   ɪd
16. started   t   d   ɪd

Practice 2

Read the following paragraphs silently. As you read, write above the underlined words how you will pronounce the -ed endings—as /t/, /d/, or /ɪd/. Then look at the words that follow these *ed* sounds. If any of these words start with a vowel sound, write linking lines between the *ed* and the vowel sound that follows. (See Lesson 5 on linking.)

After you have finished marking these paragraphs, take turns reading them aloud with a partner.

Example: They agreed it was a violent movie.

Two people went to a violent movie. One of them <u>liked</u> it a lot, and the other <u>hated</u> it. The movie <u>showed</u> a lot of blood and killing, and it <u>ended</u> with probably a hundred people dead. Of course, the person who <u>disliked</u> the movie <u>wanted</u> to leave as soon as it <u>started</u>, but he <u>agreed</u> to stay because his friend <u>wanted</u> to stay.

After the movie they <u>talked</u> for at least an hour. The guy <u>claimed</u> that all that violence <u>affected</u> the way children <u>behaved</u>, and gave them examples of how people <u>committed</u> crimes. His friend listened and said she <u>hoped</u> he was wrong.

Practice 3

Go through the dialogue in this lesson and any other lessons that you have studied. Find ten regular verbs in the past tense, and complete the chart below. After you have completed the chart, practice saying the past tense verbs and the words that come after them. Link these words when necessary.

Past Tense Verbs	Pronunciation of -ed Ending			Word that Follows	Linked?		From Chapter #
1. _____	t	d	ɪd	_____	yes	no	_____
2. _____	t	d	ɪd	_____	yes	no	_____
3. _____	t	d	ɪd	_____	yes	no	_____
4. _____	t	d	ɪd	_____	yes	no	_____
5. _____	t	d	ɪd	_____	yes	no	_____
6. _____	t	d	ɪd	_____	yes	no	_____
7. _____	t	d	ɪd	_____	yes	no	_____
8. _____	t	d	ɪd	_____	yes	no	_____
9. _____	t	d	ɪd	_____	yes	no	_____
10. _____	t	d	ɪd	_____	yes	no	_____

Practice 4: Listen and Speak

The dictations in Appendix A are all in the past tense. Choose a dictation from a lesson that you have already studied, and look for regular verbs in the past tense as you silently read it. Then, on each of these verbs, mark which of the three -ed endings you think you should use. Listen to the dictation to check, and then practice saying the past tense verbs aloud. When you are ready, dictate the paragraph or paragraphs to a partner or small group.

Practice 5: Pronunciation Review

As you read this lesson's dialogue, listen again to the tape. See if you can spot any reduced forms (see Lesson 6). There is no need to repeat the reduced forms, but there is a need for you to learn to recognize them as they are spoken by native speakers.

Review the information about thought groups and linking in Lesson 5. Then listen to this lesson's dialogue again and insert parentheses and linking lines where you think they belong. With a partner, perform the dialogue.

5. Questions for Discussion and/or Writing

(For more detailed instructions, see Lesson 1, page 13.)

> *For Discussion:* You can answer these questions orally in groups or in the *Walk and Talk* activity in Appendix B.

> *For Writing:* You can write your own answers to these questions, or you can write the responses that you received from students during the *Walk and Talk* activity.

Questions

1. Think about something that disappointed you—a trip, a movie, a restaurant, a course, etc. Then explain why it left a lot to be desired.
2. When you were a child, did your parents let you get away with murder, or were they strict? Explain.
3. From your standpoint, how should parents discipline their children—with words or by striking them physically?
4. The news media are often accused of blowing stories out of proportion. In other words, they may take a story and make it sound more important than it really is. What do you think? (If possible, give examples from the news.)
5. Explain two or three things that you have yet to do (things that you should have already done long ago).
6. Give an example of a bone of contention between you and a friend or relative. Or, if you'd rather not get too personal, give an example of a bone of contention between two politicians with different beliefs.
7. What is the most expensive thing you bought during this past year? Did you get your money's worth? Explain.
8. What drives you up the wall at home? At school? At work? In this country?

6. Write Your Own

Here are some situations along with expressions from this lesson. Use your imagination and write your own sentences or dialogues to describe, explain, or act out the situations. Try to use at least two of the expressions in parentheses.

1. A woman asks her brother how his vacation was. Unfortunately, it wasn't very good. What the hotel brochure described wasn't actually true. The hotel had many problems—the pool had no water, the room wasn't very nice, and the people in the room above made a lot of noise. Finally, he talked to the manager and told him that he was going to leave. He and his family switched to another hotel, which was much better. Write the dialogue between the sister and brother. *(leave a lot to be desired, drive someone up the wall, from my standpoint)*

Sister: _____

Brother: _____

_____

_____

_____

2. A student who is graduating from high school has decided that she really doesn't want to go to college even though her parents have always expected her to go. She knows her parents won't agree with her. But she wants to get a job and maybe go to college later. In a letter, she explains all this and asks her parents to understand and respect her decision. Write the letter to her parents. *(a foregone conclusion that, not written in stone, a bone of contention)*

Dear Mom and Dad,

_____

_____

_____

_____

Choose one of your corrected "Write Your Own" sections and dictate it to a partner or group or your entire class. Before you do this, think about the pronunciation points you have studied and mark your sentences.

7. Scene Two

Consider the opening conversation between the two friends to be the first scene of a play. On your own, with a partner, or in a small group, now write Scene Two. Imagine that they are now at a cafe after the movie. They start out trying to find a subject they agree on, but they keep getting into heated arguments (possibly about political issues, their opinions of their friends or relatives, music, sports, etc.).

As you write, see if any of the expressions from this or other lessons fit into the conversation. Also, feel free to use other expressions that you know. But don't feel that it is necessary to have an idiom in every sentence.

If possible, groups of students can practice various versions of Scene Two and then perform them for the class. You might even want to videotape these scenes.

8. Chain Story

Here is the beginning of a story. Continue the story by going around the room and having each student orally add a sentence, or get into small groups and have group members each add a sentence one by one. Try to have three to five expressions in your story. It will be helpful if the expressions from the dialogue are written on the board for all to see.

One day a person visits his/her cousin in jail. The cousin robbed a bank and tries to make excuses for it. The two cousins argue. One says. . . .

9. Role Playing

Using the new expressions from this lesson, act out the following role play. The new expressions should be written on the board.

A young brother and sister are fighting over what to watch on TV. The brother wants to watch a movie, and the sister wants to watch a sports program. They are making so much noise that their parents come in.

Possible starting line: Give me that remote control!

10. Tic Tac Toe

In this variation of tic tac toe, to get an X or an O you need to create a grammatically correct sentence that is logical in meaning. Here is a game to start you off. Create as many games as you like, using expressions from Lesson 8. And if you would like to review expressions from any other lesson that you have studied, add them to the game.

leave a lot to be desired	*have no bearing on*	*get away with*
it's not written in stone	*have yet to*	*get through to*
get one's money's worth	*drive someone up the wall*	*blow something out of proportion*

11. Expand on What You Now Know

In this lesson, you studied two-word verbs with the words *get* and *blow*. Many more expressions exist in combination with these words.

You already know:

get away with **blow** something out of proportion
through to

To learn some more expressions with these words, with a partner ask a native speaker to help you fill out this chart. In order to do this kind of assignment, see Appendix C, "Contact Assignments," for information on how to start a conversation with a native speaker of English.

Pronunciation Note: Remember to stress the second part of two-word verbs.

	Meaning	**Sample Sentence**
get		
back at	_____	_____
		_____
even with	_____	_____
		_____
along with	_____	_____
		_____
through with	_____	_____
		_____
blow		
away	_____	_____
		_____
off steam	_____	_____
		_____
open	_____	_____
		_____
over	_____	_____
		_____
up	_____	_____
		_____

12. Connect Your Class to the Real World

Every week, on your own or with a partner, find three expressions from the real world that are new to you. Keep an inventory in your notebook or on 3 x 5 cards, following the format in Appendix D, "Student Idiom Collection." Be ready to share what you found in small groups or with your entire class.

Crossword Puzzle, Lessons 7 and 8

Across

3. If I keep plugging ____ at this, maybe I'll get it.

5. Computers are a ____ leap over typewriters, aren't they?

9. There are no ifs, ands, or buts ____ it. You're absolutely right!

10. With your ability, you're ____ to become an English teacher.

Down

1. We had a great time and got ____ money's worth, that's for sure.

2. From his ____, everything is just fine.

3. People who break the law should be held ____ for their actions.

4. I've been ____ with this homework for hours. When will I be finished?

6. Today we take a lot of things for ____.

16. It's a ____ conclusion that it takes a lot of work to learn English.
18. I'm ____ a bind. Can you help me?
11. Your argument just doesn't ____ water.
13. We haven't decided yet. We're going to hold ____ for a while.
19. Sorry, but that has no ____ on what we're talking about.
20. He thought the movie ____ a lot to be desired.
21. I have ____ to meet someone here who I don't like.
22. They don't agree on that. It's a big ____ of contention between them.
23. She got very angry and blew everything out of ____.
24. It shouldn't be a bone of ____. Let's talk about it.

7. You can change it. It's not written in ____.
8. I wasn't going to do it, but you ____ me over.
12. I didn't like it at first, but it's ____ on me.
14. Do you think I can ____ you away from the TV?
15. Doesn't that noise drive you up the ____.
17. The lecture ____ on and on. I was so bored.
22. They lost their ____ and took the wrong exit.

Flying to a Distant Place— A Bad Case of Jet Lag

Warm-Up

Read the following explanation of the phenomenon of jet lag, offered by Professor Karl C. Hamner of UCLA: "After travelers fly across many time zones in a day, they are under new local times, and it takes a few days for their bodies to adjust to the new day-night patterns. This phenomenon is commonly called jet lag."

Answer the following:

Have you ever taken a long airplane trip? If yes, tell your classmates:

- where you started from and landed

- what the time difference is between where you took off from and where you landed

- whether or not you took naps at unusual times, or were awake in the middle of the night soon after your arrival

- how long it took you to adjust to the time in the country you arrived in

- your advice for travelers on how to prevent or get over jet lag

Dialogue Steps

Choose one or more of the following:
(a)   Listen to the tape as you read the dialogue.
(b)   Say the dialogue in pairs.
(c)   Have two volunteers perform the dialogue in front of the class.

(at home)

DAUGHTER: Dad, what time is it?

FATHER: Four.

DAUGHTER: Four? Who knows what time that is for me! Boy, I **have** terrible **jet lag. I can't keep my eyes open.**

FATHER: Well, I'm not going to let you go to sleep in the middle of the afternoon. Let's take a walk, and you can tell me about your trip.

DAUGHTER: I'm sorry Daddy, but **I'm** too **wiped out.** I think I'll **stretch out** and take a little nap.

FATHER: Uh-uh—no naps. You know if you go to sleep now, you're going to wake up in the middle of the night. Come on, let's take a little walk around the block. Maybe you'll **get a second wind.**

DAUGHTER: I sure hope so.

(on their walk)

DAUGHTER: I missed you and Mom a lot. A year is a long time.

FATHER: We missed you too, honey. But we knew that studying in another country was good for you.

DAUGHTER: Well, I sure **had my ups and downs.** Sometimes I even thought about coming home early, but I was determined to stick it out.*

FATHER: And I'm glad you did. What was so hard for you over there?

DAUGHTER: Oh, I don't think I can **scratch the surface.** There were times, especially in the winter, when I got really homesick. You know, it's hard to be away during holidays. But my friends were absolutely great. Especially my roommate. Remember she took me home to her family? That really helped.

FATHER: If we'd known how homesick you were, we would've **hopped on** a plane!

DAUGHTER: But that would've been too expensive. And, anyway, in the spring I got much better. **It** finally **hit home** that I was lucky to be away, living in another culture. I stopped being so **wrapped up** in my problems and **got out of my rut.** I started going to more parties, concerts, and other campus events. I worked harder in my classes, too. And listen to this! After a while, I didn't realize it, but my fluency improved. Can you imagine that there were times when I forgot I wasn't speaking English?

---
*See Lesson 3

FATHER:	**That's music to my ears!** I knew you'd do it if you lived over there.
DAUGHTER:	And **to top that off,** people started to compliment my pronunciation.
FATHER:	Wow! You don't want to lose all that. Are there any conversation classes you can take here?
DAUGHTER:	Uh—Dad, I wasn't going to **broach the subject** till later, but . . . there's a chance that I can get a scholarship and go back next year.
FATHER:	Go back? But you just got home!
DAUGHTER:	I know.
FATHER:	Do you really want to go back?
DAUGHTER:	The truth is, I'm not sure. I need to **sleep on it.** Speaking of sleep, now can I take a little nap? I'm so sleepy!

Guess the Meanings

Below is a list of paraphrases of five of the idiomatic expressions contained in the dialogue. On your own or with a partner, try to guess the five.

Paraphrase	Idiomatic Expression from the Dialogue
1. had good times and bad times	_____
2. lie down	_____
3. mention this topic	_____
4. involved in	_____
5. I finally realized	_____

■ Understanding the New Expressions

Figure It Out with Others and/or On Your Own

(For more detailed instructions, see Lesson 1, page 3.)

WITH OTHERS:

Work in small groups to go through this information. The leader of each group should make sure that everyone participates equally.

ON YOUR OWN:

Read this entire section carefully.

For each expression, circle the check mark or question mark in the margin to indicate whether or not you understand the information given.

All Clear?

√ ?   **1. háve jét lag**

Definition: feel sleepy during the day and awake at night because your body is used to a different time zone

Note 1: Jet lag occurs when people travel long distances. Although it may be 2:00 in the afternoon in the country they just arrived in, it may be nighttime in the country they just left. It usually takes a few days for the body to become used to the new time.

Note 2: *Jet lag* is often used with the following verbs: *avoid/ prevent* jet lag, *have* jet lag, *get over* jet lag.

S1: Do you know how I can **avoid jet lag?**
S2: Some people try to change the time they go to bed before they travel, but I don't know if that works.

S1: You're landing on Sunday and going to work on Monday? How is that possible? Won't you **have jet lag?**
S2: Probably, but I can do it. I usually **get over jet lag** pretty fast.

√ ?   **2. cán't kéep one's éyes ópen**

Definition: can't stay awake because one is so sleepy

S1: It's time to put the kids to bed. Look—**they can't keep their eyes open.**
S2: You're right. . . . Come on, kids, bedtime!

√ ?   **3. be wiped óut**

Definition: be very tired; exhausted

Note: This is a very informal expression.

S1: I**'m wiped out.** I spent six hours on this assignment!
S2: I'd **be wiped out** too.

Contrast: **to wipe someone óut** = to make someone tired

—The trip really **wiped me out.**
—That test **wiped me out.** I'm going to go somewhere and relax.
—Babysitting for that child always **wipes her out.**

Contrast: **to wipe something óut** = to destroy

—The soldiers **wiped out** the entire village. (The soldiers killed everyone.)
—The earthquake **wiped out** the whole area.
—Researchers are trying to find the way to **wipe out** AIDS.

Contrast the literal meaning of **"wipe out:"** clean (wipe/rub) the inside of something, usually with a cloth

—I **wiped out** the sink.

√ ? **4. stretch óut**

Definition: lie down

—I'm going to **stretch out** on the couch and take a nap.
—This couch is too short. You can't **stretch out.**

Contrast: **stretch something óut** = make something wider or longer

—Look at how far you can **stretch out** this rubber band.
—He **stretched** the story **out** with millions of details. I almost fell asleep.

Contrast: **be stretched óut**

S1: Look! My sweater **is** all **stretched out.**
S2: Did you put it in the washing machine?
S1: Uh-huh.
S2: That's why. You should've washed it by hand.

√ ? **5. gét a sécond wínd**

Definition: get new energy after being very tired

Origin Note: An athlete, such as a runner, may breathe very fast at first. When the breathing becomes regular again, it is called a *second wind.*

S1: What are you doing? I thought you said you were too tired to clean the house.
S2: I don't know. Somehow I **got a second wind.**
S1: Well, I'm glad. The house looks great.

S1: I'm full of energy. It's weird, because an hour ago I needed a nap.
S2: You **got a second wind.** But I didn't. I'm going to take a break.

√ ? 6. háve one's úps and dówns

Definition: have good and bad periods of time

S1: How's your new job?
S2: It **has its ups and downs,** but it's all right.

S1: How is she now that she's back home?
S2: She **has her ups and downs** just like she does everywhere else.

√ ? 7. scrátch the súrface

Definition: talk or write about a topic on a superficial level; not go deeply into the subject

Opposite: talk or write about something **in dépth**

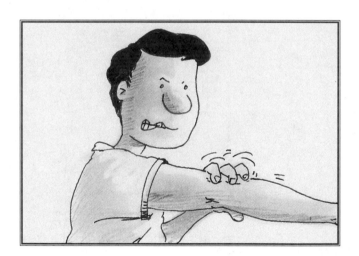

—I've told you a little about my trip. But I only **scratched the surface** because there's so much more to tell.

—When they've finished this course, many students think they've learned all there is to know about this subject. But I'm afraid that we can only **scratch the surface** here. There's so much more to learn, and we can't cover it all.

—You've only **scratched the surface** of the environmental problems we face. We need to continue this conversation and discuss each problem **in depth**.

Contrast: **from scrátch** = with the original materials; not previously prepared by someone else

—I didn't use a cake mix. I baked this cake **from scratch.**
—She didn't buy her computer. She built it **from scratch.**

√ ? **8. hóp on**

Definition: get on a plane, bus, train, motorcycle, or boat without much planning beforehand

Similar Expression: **hop ín** (a car). This expression is usually used in the imperative form: *Hop in!*

Note: These are informal expressions that are used to show that someone gets on a means of transportation somewhat spontaneously, without much planning.

Pronunciation Note: When you just say "Hop *on!*" or "Hop *in*," stress the second word.

S1: (on the phone): I need you. Can you come right away?
S2: I'll **hop on** the next plane/train/bus.

S1: When I heard what happened, I **hopped on** the first plane I could get.
S2: I'm sure they felt better when you got there.

S1: (talking through a car window to friends): Can I join you?
S2: Sure, **hop in!**

√ ? **9. it hít hóme (that)**

Definition: something finally became clear deep in one's heart or mind

—They knew they'd won the lottery, but it didn't really **hit home** until they got their first check and bought a new car.
—When it finally **hit home** that they were going to be parents, they got a little scared.
—It finally **hit home** that she'd lost her job when she woke up and had nowhere to go.

Contrast: **it (finally) hit someone that** = something made someone realize that . . .

—**It** finally **hit him that** he was really a father.
                    she was not a little girl anymore, that she had grown up.
                    he had to work harder or he'd lose his job.
                    he would never see them again.

√ ? **10. be/gét wrapped úp in**

Definition: be/get very, very involved in; give all of one's attention to

S1: Didn't you hear the phone?
S2: No. I **was** really **wrapped up in** my work, and I didn't hear a thing.

S1: She's not very friendly.
S2: No, she**'s** very **wrapped up in** herself.

Contrast: **wrap something úp** (a package or gift)

—Can you help me **wrap up** these presents? Here's the wrapping paper.
—Here, Dad. I **wrapped** this **up** for you. Open it.

√ ? 11. **gét out of one's rút**

Definition: get out of an unhappy psychological situation or boring routine

Note: A *rut* is literally a track in the ground that can cause one to get stuck.

S1: I need to **get out of this rut.** I need a big change in my life. Everything is so boring.
S2: Why don't you look for another job or take a class?

Contrast: **be in a rút**

S1: Why's he so sad?
S2: He seems to **be in a rut.** I think he needs a change, or at least a vacation.

S1: You seem much happier than you were the last time I saw you.
S2: Yeah, I'm better. I **was in a rut** then, but I've made some changes, and things are much better now.

√ ? 12. **músic to one's éars**

Definition: great news that is a pleasure to hear

S1: Mom, we're moving back home. We want the kids to grow up near you and Dad. They need to grow up near their grandparents.
S2: Oh, honey . . . that's **music to my ears!**

—When she said, "I love you," it was **music to his ears.**

Contrast: **be áll éars** = be ready and eager to listen

S1: Do you want to hear about my trip?
S2: Yes, I've been waiting. I'**m all ears.**

S1: Wait till you hear what happened!
S2: Hurry up and tell us. We'**re all ears.**

Contrast: **fáce the músic** = face the punishment

—I have to to go home now and **face the music.** My parents found out about my bad grades.

—The students were discovered cheating and were sent to the principal to **face the music.**

√ ? 13. to top thát off, ___

Definition: To add to what I have already said, here is one more thing that makes what happened before either better or worse.

Note: First you say what happened, and then you add what was unexpected.

S1: First we met at my house and had some hors d'oeuvres. Then we went to a really nice restaurant, and after that we went to the theater. And **to top that all off,** we went out for drinks afterward.
S2: Wow! What an evening!

S1: My car was stolen, I lost my books, and **to top that off,** I caught a cold.
S2: Poor kid. Your luck will change.

√ ? 14. bróach the súbject

Definition: introduce a new topic while feeling that the response from others may be negative

Origin Note: An instrument called a *broach* is used to open beer barrels. When the barrels are opened, the beer is brought to light, just as a subject has been brought to light when it is broached (brought up). *(Source: Brewers's Dictionary of Phrase & Fable)*

S1: Did you ask?
S2: No. I was afraid to **broach the subject** because they weren't in a good mood.

—I hate to **broach the subject** of money right now, but can I borrow a few dollars?

—I know you don't want me to **broach the subject,** but when are you going to get married? You're not getting any younger.

Similar Expression: **bring úp (a subject), bring (something) úp** = introduce a new topic. This expression is neutral—the response from others may not be negative. (The response when "broaching a subject" is expected to be negative.)

S1: I need to **bring up** another **subject** before the meeting is over. Do you think we'll have time?
S2: Sure. What's it about?

S1: We need to talk about salaries.
S2: I'm glad you **brought** that **up.** I almost forgot.

√ ? 15. sléep on it

Definition: not make a decision quickly; think about something and make a decision the next day or even later

S1: Will you marry me?
S2: Uh—
S1: Don't answer me now. **Sleep on it** and let me know tomorrow.

S1: Will you take the new job?
S2: I can't say yet. I need to **sleep on it** for a few days.

S1: It's a great chance for a vacation. Should I make the reservations?
S2: I don't know . . . Can I **sleep on it** and tell you tomorrow?

—I **slept on it,** and yes, I will marry you!
—She **slept on it** and decided not to take the new job.
—I **slept on it** and decided that you should go ahead and make those reservations. It sounds like a great idea for a vacation.

Similar Expression: **mull it óver** = think about something for a while

S1: Did he take the new job?
S2: Not yet. He**'s** still **mulling it over.**

S1: Do you want me to introduce you to them?
S2: Maybe . . . let me **mull it over** first.

S1: I'll give you a raise if you stay in your job.
S2: Can you give me a few days? I need to **mull it over.**

Exercises

1. Mini-Dialogues

Below are two exercises with two columns each, A and B. Column A contains the first lines of dialogues, and column B contains possible responses. For each opening line in column A, choose the *best* response from column B. Sometimes more than one response is possible. Not all responses can be used.

When checking the exercise in class, perform each mini-dialogue. One student should read an item from column A, and another student should respond with the answer from column B.

1. A
____ **1.** I thought you were tired.
____ **2.** Can I tell you a secret?
____ **3.** I think I'll stretch out and read for a while.
____ **4.** I heard he got out of the hospital. How's he doing?
____ **5.** The news just gives headlines with only a few details.
____ **6.** I'm sorry. I can't decide right now.

1. B
a. I'm all ears.
b. We made it from scratch.
c. That's for sure. They only scratch the surface of the stories.
d. Well, he has his ups and downs.
e. I was, but I got a second wind, and now I'm full of energy.
f. There's a lounge chair outside. I think you'll be very comfortable there.
g. No problem. Sleep on it and then give me a call.

2. A

_____ 1. Where have you been? I haven't seen you in a long time!

_____ 2. How was your twenty-hour trip?

_____ 3. We're getting married.

_____ 4. Can you give me a ride home?

_____ 5. I'm moving across the country. I need to get out of this rut.

_____ 6. What's wrong?

2. B

a. Great. I'm not as wiped out as I thought I'd be.

b. Don't jump on me!

c. That's music to my ears!

d. I'm afraid to broach this subject, but can I borrow a few bucks?

e. What about your family? Are you going to just pick up and go?

f. I know and I'm sorry. I've been really wrapped up in my work.

g. Sure. Hop in.

2. Choosing the Idiom

The following is a conversation between the daughter from the opening dialogue and her mother. Her mother is trying to wake her up from her nap. Fill in the blanks with the best possible expressions from the list. Pay special attention to how the expressions are used grammatically. You may need to consider verb tenses, subject-verb agreement, pronouns, active vs. passive voice, etc. Not all of the expressions in the list can be used. After you finish, practice reading the sentences aloud.

wiped out
have one's ups and downs
be all ears
scratch the surface
it hit home
to top that off

hop in
get a second wind
get over jet lag
hop on
wrapped up in
mull it over

MOTHER: Honey, wake up. Come on.

DAUGHTER: What time is it?

MOTHER: It's almost 7. You need to get ready for dinner.

DAUGHTER: I'm not hungry. Please let me sleep. I'm so (1) _____
              _____ .

MOTHER: I want to hear about your plans.

DAUGHTER: I'll tell you about them after I (2) _____ .

MOTHER: Dad says that you might go back next year. To tell you the truth,
              I want you to stay home and finish school here. We missed you so
              much when you were away.

DAUGHTER: I missed you, too. Please let me sleep.

MOTHER: On your birthday I almost (3) _____
              a plane to visit you. I wanted to surprise you.

DAUGHTER: You should've come. I would've introduced you to all my friends.

MOTHER: Tell me about them now. I (4) _____ .

DAUGHTER: Now? I'm too tired. How can I even (5) _____
              _____ ? There's so much to tell.

MOTHER: Well, you can start at the dinner table.

DAUGHTER: Dinner, dinner, dinner.

MOTHER: See! You (6) _____ now. I knew I could
              wake you up.

DAUGHTER: Let's just talk here. I don't want to get up. But *you* talk. Tell me
              about how *you've* been.

MOTHER: OK. But only for a few minutes. You know, when you first left,

              (7) _____ that you were really on your
              own. My baby had left the nest. It was hard at the beginning not

              having any kids here. I (8) _____ . One
              day I'd be fine, and the next day I'd be kind of sad. But over time

              I got (9) _____ my work. Oh, and
              I forgot to tell you—I started taking piano lessons! Can you believe

              it? Hey! Your eyes are closing. Now don't go back to sleep.

3. Dictation

Your teacher or one of your classmates will read the dictation for this lesson
from Appendix A, or you will listen to the dictation on the audio program.
You will hear the dictation three times. First, just listen. Second, as you listen,
write the dictation on a separate piece of paper. Third, check what you
have written.

4. Pronunciation—Troublesome Consonant Sounds

Choose two consonant sounds that you have difficulty producing. You might
want to refer to the list of consonant sounds in Lesson 7 on page 126-127 or
choose from the following:

Difficult Sounds	Sounds Often Used Instead of Difficult Sound	How to Produce Difficult Sound
/θ/—*th* as in *think* /ʃ/—*th* as in *this*	/t/, /s/ /d/, /z/	To produce the two *th* sounds, its necessary to put your tongue out slightly between your teeth. To produce the voiceless *th*, blow air without using your voice. To produce the voiced *th*, use your voice but don't blow air. If you don't put your tongue between your teeth, you will get a /t/ or /s/ sound for the voiceless *th* or a /d/ or /z/ sound for the voiced *th*.
 /v/ as in *very* /f/ as in *ferry*	/b/	To produce the /v/ and /f/ sounds, it is necessary to put your top front teeth on your lower lip. To produce the voiceless /f/ sound, blow air without using your voice. To produce the voiced *v* sound, don't blow air and use your voice. If you don't put your top teeth on your lower lip, your two lips will touch and produce a /b/ sound instead.
/l/ as in *lag* /r/ as in *rag*	/r/ /l/	To produce the /l/ sound, touch the tip of your tongue against the tooth ridge behind your top front teeth. To produce the /r/ sound, don't let the tip of your tongue touch the tooth ridge. With the /r/, it's OK if the sides of your tongue touch your side teeth. Also with the /r/, make a circle with your lips.

/n/ as in *nag*	/l/	The /n/ sound is similar to the /l/ sound, but with the /n/, you should release air through your nose. Also, the /l/ is produced with the very tip of the tongue against the tooth ridge behind the top front teeth, while with the /n/, more of the tip of the tongue is pressed against the tooth ridge.

Practice 1

Go back to the first dialogue in this lesson. As you read silently, look for words that contain the consonant sounds that you have chosen to focus on. These sounds may appear at the beginning, in the middle, or at the ends of words. Circle these words and then list them below:

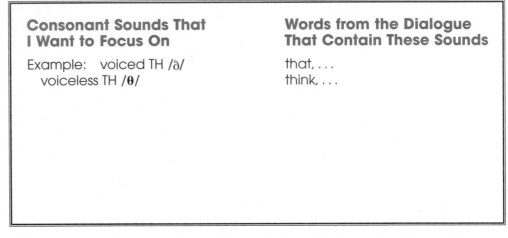

Consonant Sounds That I Want to Focus On	**Words from the Dialogue That Contain These Sounds**
Example: voiced TH /ð/ voiceless TH /θ/	that, . . . think, . . .

Practice saying these words and, if possible, look into a mirror to see, for example, if your tongue and/or teeth are where they should be.

Practice 2

Choose three sentences from the dialogue that contain the sounds that you are focusing on. Dictate these sentences to your partner.

Practice 3: Listen and Speak

As you read this lesson's dialogue, listen to the tape and pay special attention to how the speakers are producing the sounds that you are focusing on. Then perform the dialogue with a partner. Give special attention to the sounds in the words that you have circled.

You can follow this procedure with any dialogue that you choose.

Practice 4

Have you ever had a misunderstanding with anyone because of your mispronunciation of a consonant sound in English (such as *tree* vs. *three*)? If yes, explain what happened. When you speak, try to make a clear distinction between the two consonant sounds that caused you trouble.

Practice 5: Pronunciation Review

Silently read the conversation between the mother and daughter (Exercise 2). As you read, circle *s* and *ed* endings and write down how they should be pronounced. (See Lessons 7 and 8.) Decide whether any of these words should be linked to the words that follow them. Practice saying these words and then perform the dialogue with a partner.

5. Questions for Discussion and/or Writing

(For more detailed instructions, see Lesson 1, page 13.)

> *For Discussion:* You can answer these questions orally in groups or in the *Walk and Talk* activity in Appendix B.

> *For Writing:* You can write your own answers to these questions, or you can write the responses that you received from students during the *Walk and Talk* activity.

Questions

1. Have you ever had jet lag? If yes, where were you? What did you do to stay awake? If you were awake when everyone else was sleeping, what did you do?
2. Describe a time when you were so wiped out that you couldn't keep your eyes open. Also explain whether or not you got a second wind.
3. If you are living in a foreign culture, or if you have ever lived in a foreign culture, describe some of the ups and downs that you have experienced.
4. If you cook, do you generally prefer to make things from scratch or to buy items that make your work easier? Explain. (An example would be a cake mix. With a mix, you could bake a cake very easily and quickly, but if you bake a cake from scratch, you would have to supply all the ingredients.)
5. What is something that you can get completely wrapped up in? Explain. (Possibilities include work, a good book, your family, political issues.)
6. What are some kinds of decisions that you would not want to make very quickly? In other words, when might you say, "I can't make that decision now. I have to sleep on it"?

6. Write Your Own

Here are some situations along with expressions from this lesson. Use your imagination and write your own sentences or dialogues to describe, explain, or act out the situations. Try to use at least two of the expressions in parentheses.

1. A student is studying for a test. She is very tired but can't go to bed yet because there is so much material to study. She is thinking about taking a little rest. Write her thoughts. (*scratch the surface, be wiped out, can't keep one's eyes open, stretch out, get a second wind*)

_____

_____

_____

_____

_____

2. Your friend is unhappy in his job. He wants to talk to you about it, and you are very willing to listen. He explains that the job is boring, that he's not learning anything new. He wants to look for another job. You advise him to carefully consider his decision. Write the dialogue between you and your friend. *(be all ears, be in a rut, sleep on it)*

Your Friend: _____

You: _____

_____

_____

_____

3. An eighteen-year-old is telling her father that she wants to move out of the house and get an apartment with her friends. Once in the past she mentioned the idea of moving out, and he was against it. She now explains that the apartment is great—not expensive, in a good neighborhood, and very close to a local college. Her father is still against this idea—he wants her to continue living at home. She asks him to at least think about it. Write the dialogue between the girl and her father. *(broach the subject, to top that off, mull it over)*

Girl: _____

Father: _____

_____

_____

_____

Choose one of your corrected "Write Your Own" sections and dictate it to a partner or group or your entire class. Before you do this, think about the pronunciation points you have studied and mark your sentences.

7. Scene Three

Consider the opening conversation between the father and daughter to be the first scene of a play, and the conversation between the mother and daughter in Exercise 2 to be the second scene. On your own, with a partner, or in a small group, now write Scene Three. Imagine that the father, mother, and daughter are sitting around their dinner table talking about the daughter's trip and the news in the neighborhood. (The daughter is now quite awake—she has her second wind.)

As you write, see if any of the expressions from this or other lessons fit into the conversation. Also, feel free to use other expressions that you know. But don't feel that it is necessary to have an idiom in every sentence.

If possible, groups of students can practice various versions of Scene Three and then perform them for the class. You might even want to videotape these scenes.

8. Chain Story

Here is the beginning of a story. Continue the story by going around the room and having each student orally add a sentence, or get into small groups and have group members each add a sentence one by one. Try to have three to five expressions in your story. It will be helpful if the expressions from the dialogue are written on the board for all to see.

One day a student started a new school. She had just arrived from another country the day before and had jet lag. The teacher told the student that she looked very tired. . . .

9. Role Playing

Using the new expressions from this lesson, act out the following role play. The new expressions should be written on the board.

Two people who work for the United Nations have just arrived in another country for a big world conference. They are talking in the hotel lobby. The opening session (meeting) will take place in two hours, but these people aren't sure that they have enough energy to go after their long trip.

Possible starting lines: Do you think you have enough energy to go to the opening session? Do you know what time it is at home right now?

10. Tic Tac Toe

In this variation of tic tac toe, to get an X or an O you need to create a grammatically correct sentence that is logical in meaning. Here is a game to start you off. Create as many games as you like, using expressions from Lesson 9. And if you would like to review expressions from any other lesson that you have studied, add them to the game.

be wiped out	stretch out	from scratch
it hit home	be wrapped up in	to top that off
broach the subject	sleep on it	mull it over

11. Expand on What You Now Know

In this lesson, you studied two-word verbs with the words *wipe, wrap,* and *sleep.* Many more expressions exist in combination with these words.

You already know:

wiped out   **wrapped** up (in)   **sleep** on it

To learn some more expressions with these words, with a partner ask a native speaker to help you fill out this chart. In order to do this kind of assignment, see Appendix C, "Contact Assignments," for information on how to start a conversation with a native speaker of English.

Pronunciation Note: Remember to stress the second part of two-word verbs.

	Meaning	Sample Sentence
wipe		
off	_____	_____
		_____
wrap		
around	_____	_____
		_____
sleep		
in	_____	_____
		_____
something off	_____	_____
		_____
over	_____	_____
		_____
through	_____	_____
		_____

12. Connect Your Class to the Real World

Every week, on your own or with a partner, find three expressions from the real world that are new to you. Keep an inventory in your notebook or on 3 x 5 cards, following the format in Appendix D, "Student Idiom Collection." Be ready to share what you found in small groups or with your entire class.

Embarrassed—
Going Through the Floor

Warm-Up

Without reading the dialogue, look at the cartoon and predict what embarrassing situation might be developing:

Predictions:

_____

_____

_____

Dialogue Steps

Choose one or more of the following:
(a) Listen to the tape as you read the dialogue.
(b) Say the dialogue in pairs.
(c) Have two volunteers perform the dialogue in front of the class.

(Part 1)
MAN: So, how are things going at work these days?

WOMAN: Could be better. Did I tell you I have a new boss? She drives me absolutely crazy.

MAN:	What does she do?
WOMAN:	Oh, she's so hard to work with. She's so unpleasant and keeps giving me a lot of work that she wants done right away. I can't tell you how exhausted I am when I get home every day.
MAN:	Have you thought about talking to her?
WOMAN:	I tried once. But it **was in vain.** She didn't listen. In fact, she talked for **a good five minutes!** I couldn't **get a word in edgewise.** All she could talk about was how it was her responsibility to make sure that things didn't **get fouled up,** and that I would have to learn to work under pressure. She**'s under the illusion that** she's a good manager.
MAN:	I wonder where she got that idea. Sorry, **go on.**
WOMAN:	Well, while we were talking, the phone rang, and she told me that something had **come up** and that I should get back to work. She can be so impolite. She really **gets to** me.

(Part 2)

WOMAN:	Oh, no!
MAN:	What's wrong? **You look like you've seen a ghost!**
WOMAN:	That's my boss! I'm going to **go through the floor.** This is truly the worst moment of my entire life.
MAN:	Calm down. Maybe she didn't hear what you said.
WOMAN:	**I will never live this down.**
MAN:	Hey, take it easy!
WOMAN:	She heard every word I said. What am I going to do?
MAN:	Maybe she needed to hear it. You said she isn't a very good listener.
WOMAN:	How can I ever go back to work? She's going to **hold a grudge against** me, and things will get even worse. I really **put my foot in my mouth** this time.
MAN:	Come on, **knock it off.** You're making it worse than it really is. When you get back to the office, you can go and talk to her and try to **straighten things out.**
WOMAN:	Oh, I could just **kick myself.**
MAN:	Listen, just take a deep breath. **It's over and done with.** I'm sure she's embarrassed too, and you know, she may even think about what you said. You never know—things could get better at the office.

Guess the Meanings

Below is a list of paraphrases of five of the idiomatic expressions contained in the dialogue. On your own or with a partner, try to guess the five.

Paraphrase	Idiomatic Expression from the Dialogue
1. continue	_____
2. never forgive me	_____
3. stop it	_____
4. was useless	_____
5. fix things	_____

■ Understanding the New Expressions

Figure It Out with Others and/or On Your Own

(For more detailed instructions, see Lesson 1, page 3.)

WITH OTHERS:

Work in small groups to go through this information. The leader of each group should make sure that everyone participates equally.

ON YOUR OWN:

Read this entire section carefully.

For each expression, circle the check mark or question mark in the margin to indicate whether or not you understand the information given.

All Clear?

√ ?

1. (be) in váin

Definition: (be) without success, without getting what was wanted

Spelling Note: Don't confuse *vain* and *vein*. A *vein* (pronounced the same as *vain*) carries blood from parts of the body to the heart; veins are the blue lines that you can see under your skin.

—He tried to get his friend to believe him, but all his efforts **were in vain** because his friend just wouldn't accept the truth.
—The rescuers worked **in vain** to reach the victims of the fire, but it was already too late.
—She called out **in vain,** but no one heard her.
—All of your efforts **were not in vain.** Look at how successful you are today!

Contrast: **be váin** = be extremely concerned about one's appearance

—People who **are vain** spend a lot of time in front of a mirror.

√ ?

2. a góod ____ mínutes/hóurs/wéeks/mónths/yéars

Definition: a full (number of) minutes/hours/weeks/months/years

Note: This expression is used to emphasize that something takes more time than might originally be expected.

—It took her **a good hour** to get the courage to ask him to marry her.
—I spent **a good five hours** on my homework.
—They spent **a good ten years** working on their house, and now look at it! They still have more work to do.

√ ? 3. gét a wórd in édgewise

Definition: say something when someone else is talking a lot

Note: I couldn't get a word in edgewise is the most common way this expression is used. It means that "someone else was talking so much that I couldn't even speak."

S1: Did you tell them at dinner?
S2: I tried, but they were all talking at once, and I couldn't **get a word in edgewise.** I'll tell them tomorrow.

S1: Excuse me for interrupting, but everyone is talking and I can't **get a word in edgewise.** Can I say something now?
S2: Sure. Sorry about that.

√ ? 4. gét/be fouled úp

Definition: get or be messed up or spoiled (ruined)

Sports Note: A *foul* in sports can be a violation of the rules. A *foul ball* occurs when a ball goes outside the lines.

S1: Why are you still home?
S2: Our plans **got fouled up,** so we decided to go tomorrow instead.

S1: The computers are down in the office, so everything **is fouled up.**
S2: Sounds like time to take a break.

Contrast: **foul (something) úp** = make a mistake or do something wrong (verb)

S1: Where's the report?
S2: I **fouled it up.** I'm sorry. I'll get it to you by tomorrow.

—Sorry I **fouled up** the plans. Can I take you out to dinner instead?

Contrast: **a fóul-up** = a mistake, something that went wrong (noun)

S1: Where are they?
S2: There was **a foul-up.** They'll be here on the next plane.

—Their wedding reception went OK even though there were a lot of **foul-ups.**

√ ? 5. be under the illúsion (that)

Definition: believe that something is a certain way when it really isn't

Idiomatic Synonym: **be under the impréssion (that)**

Note: An illusion is a false perception (understanding) of reality.

S1: Her parents **were under the illusion that** she was studying all the time, but in reality she was always out with her boyfriend.

S2: What did they do when they found out?

S1: At first I **was under the illusion that** English was easy, but now I know otherwise.

S2: I always knew it would be hard. Why did you start out thinking it would be easy?

√ ? 6. go ón

Definition: continue

—Sorry about the phone interruption. We can **go on** with our work now.
—**Go on.** I didn't mean to interrupt you.
—The concert **went on** and **on,** and I thought it would never end.

Contrast other definitions of "*go on*":

What's **going ón**? = What's happening?
There's a party **going ón** across the street. = There's a party happening.
Don't wait for me. **Go ón.** = Hurry! Leave without me; go.
Oh, **go ón!** I don't believe you. = I think you're joking.
The lights **go ón** automatically when it gets dark. = The lights turn on.

√ ? 7. come úp

Definition: occur unexpectedly and interfere with plans

S1: Listen, I can't meet you on Saturday. Something has **come up.** Would Sunday be possible?
S2: No problem.

S1: They were supposed to be here at 2:00, but something **came up.** They asked if they could come at 3:00. Would that be OK?
S2: What can I say?

√ ? 8. gét to someone

Definition: bother someone

S1: Did you see the way they talked to him? They were really rude.
S2: They're always that way. The way they act **gets to** me.

S1: I wish you'd stop complaining. It really **gets to** me.
S2: Sorry.

Contrast: **gét to** = reach or affect a person emotionally

—That story really **got to** me. I can't stop thinking about it.
—The look on the child's face **got to** me. I'll never forget it.

Contrast: **gét to** = arrive at a place

—When will we **get to** San Francisco?

√ ? 9. You lóok like you've séen a ghóst!

Definition: You look very shocked.

S1: What's wrong with you? **You look like you've seen a ghost!**
S2: I need to sit down. I just had a big shock.

√ ? **10. gó through the flóor**

Definition: (be so embarrassed that you want to) disappear so no one will see you

Idiomatic Synonym: **blénd into the wóodwork**

—As soon as I realized that I had said the wrong thing, I wanted to **go through the floor.** (I wanted to **blend into the woodwork.**)
—When they walked into the party in blue jeans, they wanted to **go through the floor** because everyone else was dressed formally.

√ ? **11. (I) will néver líve this dówn.**

Definition: I will never get over this embarrassment. (And people will never forget my big mistake, and I will always be extremely embarrassed about it.)

—I got lost on my way to my wedding. **I will never live this down.**
—They found out what we really think of them? **We'll never live this down.**
—I gave a speech in front of the whole class, and my pants were ripped and everyone saw? **I'll never live this down!**

√ ? **12. hóld/háve a grúdge (against someone)**

Definition: have a deep feeling of resentment against someone because of something upsetting that happened in the past

S1: Don't you think it's bad to **hold a grudge**? I think people need to forgive each other.
S2: So do I, but that's often easier said than done.

S1: Why does she **have a grudge against** her old friend?
S2: You haven't heard? Because her old "friend" is going out with her boyfriend.
S1: Oh, I see.

√ ? **13. pút one's fóot in one's móuth**

Definition: unintentionally say something that causes someone else to feel pain or embarrassment

Note: This expression is often used *after* an embarrassing situation occurs, when someone tells someone else about what had happened.

S1: Are you going to be at their party on Saturday?
S2: I . . . I wasn't invited.
S1: Oops! I was sure you would be.
Later:
S1: I asked her if she'd be at their party and she said she wasn't invited. I really **put my foot in my mouth.** I didn't know what to say!
S3: Don't worry about it. They should've invited her. Maybe they forgot.

S1: Don't take a class with that teacher. He's terrible.
S2: He's my father.
S1: Uh-oh! I think I just **put my foot in my mouth!**

√ ?   **14. knock it óff**

Definition: stop it

Note: This is a very informal expression that should be used only with people you know well.

Embarrassed—Going Through the Floor

—Come on, you two. **Knock it off!** You've been arguing too much.

—**Knock it off** in there. You're making too much noise, and I can't sleep.

√ ? 15. straighten things óut

Definition: fix things after there has been a problem, confusion, a mistake, or a misunderstanding

Idiomatic Synonym: **cléar the áir**

Note: straighten things out and clear the air mean the same thing only in cases in which there is anger between people.

(situations in which anger is a factor)
S1: We haven't talked to each other in a week.
S2: Don't you think it's time to **straighten things out (clear the air)?**
S1: I guess you're right.

S1: I'm tired of this. I don't want us to be mad at each other.
S2: Neither do I. Let's **straighten things out (clear the air).** First, you tell me what I did to make you angry.

(situation in which anger is not a factor)
S1: What am I going to do? I thought my paper wasn't due till next week! And it's due today!
S2: It was an honest misunderstanding. Maybe you can **straighten things out** by talking to the teacher.

√ ? 16. could kíck oneself (for)

Definition: regret doing something

S1: What's wrong?
S2: I could **kick myself!** I just told him about the surprise party!

—I could **kick myself for** say**ing** that.
—There are no more seats left. I could **kick myself for** not mak**ing** reservations.

√ ? **17. It's óver and dóne with.**

Definition: It's permanently finished (and you can't do anything about it).

S1: I'm so sorry about what I did yesterday.
S2: Don't worry. **It's over and done with.** Today's a new day.

S1: Why did I mail that letter?
S2: **It's over and done with.** There's nothing you can do about it, so try to forget about it. Or: Don't cry over spilt milk. It's over and done with. (See Lesson 6.)

Exercises

1. Mini-Dialogues

Below are two exercises with two columns each, A and B. Column A contains the first lines of dialogues, and column B contains possible responses. For each opening line in column A, choose the best response from column B. Sometimes more than one response is possible. Not all responses can be used.

When checking the exercise in class, perform each mini-dialogue. One student should read an item from column A, and another student should respond with the answer from column B.

1. A

____ **1.** Come on, knock it off. What are you two arguing about, anyway?
____ **2.** I was so frustrated. They didn't stop talking.
____ **3.** Why are you so late?
____ **4.** What happened? You look like you've seen a ghost!
____ **5.** He's mad at me.

1. B

a. My first flight was delayed, and then I missed my connecting flight. Everything got all fouled up.
b. He told me he was so embarrassed, he wanted to go through the floor.
c. What are you going to do to straighten things out?
d. I know what you mean. No one could get a word in edgewise.
e. It's between us.
f. You won't believe what I just saw in my closet!

2. A

____ **1.** That movie got to me. I've been thinking about it all day.
____ **2.** I was under the illusion that he was doctor. But he's still in medical school.
____ **3.** We missed you at the party last night.
____ **4.** Those two families have had a grudge against each other for years.
____ **5.** I could kick myself for what I said. Now I'm in big trouble.

2. B

a. That's interesting. It didn't do a thing for me.
b. Sorry about that. Something important came up.
c. What do you think will happen to you?
d. I put my foot in my mouth.
e. What started it?
f. Why are you so surprised?

2. Choosing the Idiom

The following is a conversation between two puppets in a puppet show. They are servants for a king in an imaginary country. Fill in the blanks with the best possible expressions from the list. Pay special attention to how the expressions are used grammatically. You may need to consider verb tenses, subject-verb agreement, pronouns, active vs. passive voice, etc. Not all of the expressions in the list can be used. After you finish, practice reading the sentences aloud.

I will never live this down   hold a grudge against
straighten things out   go on
be in vain   under the impression
for a good   get a word in edgewise
put one's foot in one's mouth   knock it off

PUPPET 1: What am I going to do? I (1) _____ !

PUPPET 2: What happened?

PUPPET 1: I criticized the king, and he overheard! (2) _____

_____ .

PUPPET 2: What exactly did you say?

PUPPET 1: I said that he talked so much, no one could (3) _____

_____ .

PUPPET 2: Are you sure he heard you?

PUPPET 1: Positive! He was standing right by the kitchen door. What am I going to do when I see him?

PUPPET 2: Don't worry . . . you may never see him again. He'll probably fire you.

PUPPET 1: Please don't say that! What am I going to do? I need this job. And I've been good to him. I follow his orders and do my job very well. I know he likes my work.

PUPPET 2: Then why don't you make an appointment to see him and try to

(4) _____ ?

PUPPET 1:   Make an appointment to see the king? But I'm only a servant!

PUPPET 2:   You're (5) _____ that the king won't talk to you, but I bet he will. Sometimes he can be a nice guy. Give it a try.

PUPPET 1:   What would I say?

PUPPET 2:   I don't know. Why don't you pretend that I'm the king and practice with me?

PUPPET 1:   OK. Let's see. Your highness ... I have come to apologize for criticizing you. I hope that you won't (6) _____ me. When I said what I said, I was having a bad day. I have worked here (7) _____ ten years and don't want to leave. I hope you will forgive me and not fire me. How's that?

PUPPET 2:   Sounds good to me, but I can't tell you for sure how the king will react. Are you ready to go see him?

PUPPET 1:   Ready? You must be kidding!

3. Dictation

Your teacher or one of your classmates will read the dictation for this lesson from Appendix A, or you will listen to the dictation on the audio program. You will hear the dictation three times. First, just listen. Second, as you listen, write the dictation on a separate piece of paper. Third, check what you have written.

4. Pronunciation—Troublesome Vowel Sounds

While there are five *letters* of the alphabet that are called vowels, in reality there are fifteen vowel *sounds.* All vowel sounds are voiced. Your tongue does not touch any particular part of your mouth when you form a vowel sound. If your tongue does touch a part of your mouth, you will be producing a consonant sound.

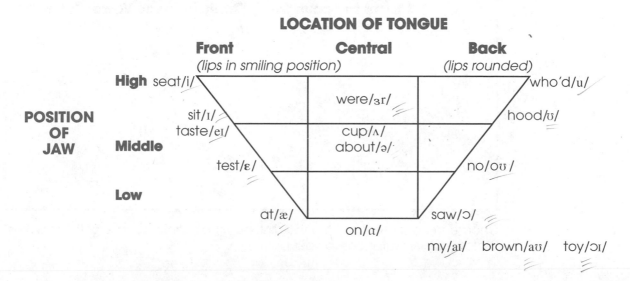

LOCATION OF TONGUE

Front (lips in smiling position) · Central · Back (lips rounded)

POSITION OF JAW

High — seat/i/ · were/ɜr/ · who'd/u/ · hood/ʊ/
Middle — sit/ɪ/ · taste/eɪ/ · cup/ʌ/ about/ə/ · no/oʊ/ · test/ɛ/
Low — at/æ/ · on/ɑ/ · saw/ɔ/
my/aɪ/ brown/aʊ/ toy/ɔɪ/

Practice 1

Put your hand under your jaw and say the "front vowel" sounds. Notice how your jaw lowers with each sound. Then do the same with the central and back vowels.

Practice 2

Say the following vowel sounds. Stretch each sound out for as long as you can.

/i/	/eɪ/	/u/	/oʊ/
eeee (seat)	ay (taste)	ooo (who'd)	oh (no)

You can say these vowel sounds for a long time. They are called "tense" vowels and are produced when the muscles of the mouth are tight, or tense.

Practice 3

Say the following vowel sounds. If you say them correctly, you will not be able to stretch them out for a long time.

/ɪ/ (sit)   /ɜr/(were)   /ʊ/ (hood)
/ɛ/ (test)   /ə/ (about)
/æ/ (at)   /ɑ/ (on)   / ɔ /(saw)

These are called "lax" vowels. They are produced when the muscles of the mouth are relaxed, not tense. If you tend to make any of these vowels tense, you end up using one of the tense vowels instead.

Practice 4

Choose two or three vowel sounds that you have difficulty pronouncing. Then go back to the first dialogue in this lesson. As you read silently, see if you can spot any words with the vowel sounds you have chosen to focus on. You may need help from a native speaker to do this. Circle these words and list them below:

	Vowel Sounds That I Want to Focus On	Words from the Dialogue That Contain These Vowel Sounds
Example:	/aʊ/	fouled up, down, . . .
	/i/	these, . . .
	/ɪ/	with, . . .

Choose three sentences from the dialogue that contain some of these words. Dictate these sentences to your partner.

Practice 5

Have you ever had a misunderstanding with anyone because of your mispronunciation of a vowel sound in English (such as sheep vs. *ship*)? If yes, explain what happened. When you speak, try to make a clear distinction between the two vowel sounds that caused you trouble.

Practice 6: Listen and Speak

Listen again to the tape of this lesson's dialogue, and pay special attention to how the speakers are producing the sounds that you are focusing on. Practice saying words with these sounds aloud.

Practice 7: Pronunciation Review

Look back at the consonant sounds you chose to focus on in Lesson 9. Circle words with those sounds in Exercise 2 of this lesson, and then practice saying the Exercise 2 dialogue with a partner. You might also want to circle words with the vowel sounds that you have chosen to work on.

5. Questions for Discussion and/or Writing

(For more detailed instructions, see Lesson 1, page 13.)

> *For Discussion:* You can answer these questions orally in groups or in the *Walk and Talk* activity in Appendix B.
>
> *For Writing:* You can write your own answers to these questions or you can write the responses that you received from students during the *Walk and Talk* activity.

Questions

1. Although it may be painful, try to think of a time when you wanted to go through the floor. What happened?
2. Is there anyone in your family who talks so much that you can't get a word in edgewise? If yes, how do you handle this person?
3. Describe a time when your plans to do something got fouled up.
4. What kind of behavior gets to you?
5. What is something that you could kick yourself for doing?
6. What do you think is the best way for people who have had a disagreement to straighten things out?

6. Write Your Own

Here are some situations along with expressions from this lesson. Use your imagination and write your own sentences or dialogues to describe, explain, or act out the situations. Try to use at least two of the expressions in parentheses.

1. Last night a group of people were having a conversation in a restaurant. During that conversation, a member of the group was telling jokes about men who wear toupees (hairpieces for men). Then, suddenly, one of the men who was listening took off his toupee and showed his bald head. The person who had been joking was extremely embarrassed. Write what that person told his or her friend the next day. (*go through the floor, could have kicked myself, put one's foot in one's mouth*)

_____

_____

_____

_____

_____

2. Your teacher has given you an assignment that you have been working on for two weeks, but you can't seem to finish it on time (you've tried, but you can't meet the deadline), and you want to do well. You go to the teacher and ask for an extension (a few more days to work). Write what you say to the teacher. *(a good ____ weeks, in vain, get fouled up)*

_____

_____

_____

_____

_____

3. You're in a very bad mood today. This is the second day that you're at home waiting for someone to come fix your sink, but he or she hasn't shown up yet. Yesterday no one came because there had been an unexpected problem. Write what has happened and what you will do. *(come up, get to, straighten things out)*

_____

_____

_____

_____

_____

Choose one of your corrected "Write Your Own" sections and dictate it to a partner or group or your entire class. Before you do this, think about the pronunciation points you have studied and mark your sentences.

7. Scene Two

Consider the opening conversation between the woman and the man to be the first scene of a play. On your own, with a partner, or in a small group, now write Scene Two. Imagine that the woman has gone back to work to straighten things out with her boss, and she now goes into her office to apologize to her.

As you write, see if any of the expressions from this or other lessons fit into the conversation. Also, feel free to use other expressions that you know. But don't feel that it is necessary to have an idiom in every sentence.

If possible, groups of students can practice various versions of Scene Two and then perform them for the class. You might even want to videotape these scenes.

8. Chain Story

Here is the beginning of a story. Continue the story by going around the room and having each student orally add a sentence, or get into small groups and have group members each add a sentence one by one. Try to have three to five expressions in your story. It will be helpful if the expressions from the dialogue are written on the board for all to see.

One day the king was talking to a friend about the queen. He didn't realize that the queen was nearby, listening to the conversation. . . .

9. Role Playing

Using the new expressions from this lesson, act out the following role play. The new expressions should be written on the board.

Two teenagers are sitting in a tree, talking about one of their friends who is not doing well in school. They don't realize that this friend is also in the tree, a little bit higher up.

After a little while, the two teenagers climb down from the tree and walk away. When they look back, they are very surprised to see their friend in the tree, and they are upset when they realize that he heard their whole conversation about him. They talk to each other about how embarrassed they feel.

Possible starting line: Oh no! Look! He heard everything we said!

10. Tic Tac Toe

In this variation of tic tac toe, to get an X or an O you need to create a grammatically correct sentence that is logical in meaning. Here is a game to start you off. Create as many games as you like, using expressions from Lesson 10. And if you would like to review expressions from any other lesson that you have studied, add them to the game.

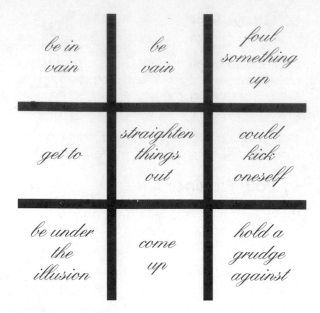

11. Expand on What You Now Know

In this lesson, you studied a two-word verb with the word *go*. Many more expressions exist in combination with this word.

You already know: **go** on

To learn some more expressions with go, with a partner ask a native speaker to help you fill out this chart. In order to do this kind of assignment, see Appendix C, "Contact Assignments," for information on how to start a conversation with a native speaker of English.

Pronunciation Note: Remember to stress the second part of two-word verbs.

go	**Meaning**	**Sample Sentence**
after	_____	_____
		_____
along with	_____	_____
		_____
back on	_____	_____
		_____
for	_____	_____
		_____
in for	_____	_____
		_____

off	_____	_____
		_____
off like clockwork	_____	_____
		_____
out on a limb	_____	_____
		_____
under	_____	_____
		_____

12. Connect Your Class to the Real World

Every week, on your own or with a partner, find three expressions from the real world that are new to you. Keep an inventory in your notebook or on 3 x 5 cards, following the format in Appendix D, "Student Idiom Collection." Be ready to share what you found in small groups or with your entire class.

Crossword Puzzle, Lessons 9 and 10

Across

2. I wasn't very happy when you ____ up that subject again.
4. We all have our ups and ____ .
6. Can you knock ____ off? It's too noisy in there.
7. They tried, but their efforts were ____ vain.

Down

1. Do you have a grudge ____ me?
3. She needs a new job. She wants to get out of her ____.
5. He said he ____ on it and made his decision.
9. The boring movie ____ on and on and on.

8. I have to sleep ____ it. I'll tell you tomorrow.
9. Can you ____ this gift up before we leave?
12. I baked this cake from ____.
14. She was so tired that she ____ keep her eyes open.
15. When the baby cried, it finally hit ____ that they were parents.
17. Everyone was talking so much that it was hard to get a word in ____.
21. I forgot! Oh, I could kick ____.
24. Tell me about it. I'm all ____.
26. You need to talk to him to ____ things out.
27. I know you don't want me to ____ the subject, but I have to.
28. If you want a ride, ____ in.
30. It took a ____ hour to get a taxi.
31. I need to ____ out for a few minutes. I'm really tired.

10. You're always so ____ up in your work. Take a break.
11. I ____ a bad case of jet lag, but I'm OK now.
12. We've been talking for two hours, and we've hardly ____ the surface.
13. Everything got ____ up. We went to the wrong restaurant.
16. She can't tell you now. She has to ____ it over.
19. I was under the ____ that everything was OK, but it wasn't.
20. When I heard the news, I said it was ____ to my ears.
22. What's wrong? You look like you've ____ a ghost!
23. Uh-oh! I really put my ____ in my mouth again.
25. He was so embarrassed that he wanted to go ____ the floor.
29. Maybe if I rest for a while, I'll ____ a second wind.

Dictations for Exercise 3

Lesson 1

Two guys, Al and Bill, were at a party. Al noticed that something was bothering Bill, and he asked him what was wrong. At first, Bill didn't want to say, but then he admitted that there was a woman he wanted to talk to, but he didn't have the guts to start a conversation. Al encouraged him to give it a shot, but Bill wouldn't go over to her. He revealed his lack of confidence in himself when he said that she wouldn't want to be caught dead with him. But Al persisted, and Bill finally admitted that he should take the initiative and walk over to her. He realized that if he passed up this chance, he'd never forgive himself.

Lesson 2

Two smokers were talking on a balcony. The woman asked the man if he was fed up with being sent outside to smoke, and she complained that she was made to feel like a criminal by nonsmokers who got up in arms when she smoked.

The woman then gave an example of a situation in which a nonsmoker showed that he looked down on her. One rainy day at work she was holding a pack of cigarettes as she was waiting for an elevator. This nonsmoker walked up and asked why she couldn't do without "those things." She was completely taken aback that he would say such a thing, but she let it slide.

Lesson 3

After class, two college students were talking at a cafe. One of them talked about how bored to death she was in one of her classes. She explained that she would stick it out because the class was required, but complained that the professor didn't know how to spark students' interest.

The other student listened to her, and then told her about an exciting history class that he was taking. It was so exciting, in fact, that he was always on the edge of his seat. He explained that his professor showed her enthusiasm for the subject, and led exciting class discussions.

He admitted that at the beginning of the semester he had been fooling around a lot and even bombed a test. But he finally buckled down and worked hard, and found that he was really enjoying his class.

Lesson 4

In an interview with a reporter, a homeless man revealed a great deal about his past. He admitted that if his parents knew that he was living on the streets, they would roll over in their graves.

The reporter was surprised to learn that the man had a college degree, and that he had once worked for a big company. Although he had had some trouble keeping up with all the work that they piled on him, he kept moving up the ladder. The problem was, however, that he was getting burned out and had no time for his family.

Eventually his wife left him, and then the company he had worked so hard for closed down. He ended up homeless.

Lesson 5

A guy, Michael, who just won ten million dollars in the lottery, went into work to give out gifts to his friends. He admitted that winning all that money was beyond his comprehension and that it really hadn't sunk in yet. He also admitted that he had no idea what was in store for him, but he was going to make sure that the money wouldn't go down the drain.

When someone asked if he was going to quit his job, he said he didn't know yet, but that he wouldn't rule it out. His friends advised him to be on the lookout for people who wanted to take advantage of him, and he promised them that he would be very careful.

Lesson 6

Mr. Claustrophobia (Mr. C.) and Mrs. Calm were surprised to find themselves stuck in an elevator. While Mr. C. complained a lot and showed his fear, Mrs. Calm tried to calm him down.

In fact, when Mr. C. told her that he was at the end of his rope and that he didn't know what he would do if he was going to be cooped up in the elevator for a long time, Mrs. Calm told him not to lose his head. She told him that they would have to make do until help arrived, and that they were lucky to have both light and company. To avoid dwelling on the scary situation they were in, Mrs. Calm encouraged Mr. C. to tell her his life story.

Lesson 7

Mom and Dad talked about how proud they were of their daughter's ability to use a computer and other forms of technology. They then admitted that they often found themselves grappling with computer programs, and that they needed help.

After taking some computer classes, Dad was plugging away at the computer all the time. He said that nothing could tear him away. Mom admitted that she preferred having a teacher to reading an instruction manual, and even suggested that they buy a modem so that they would be able to get online. They were surprised at how interested in technology their family had become.

Lesson 8

Two friends went to a movie. One felt that it was nothing to write home about, while the other loved it. The one who didn't like the movie felt that it had too much violence and that the violence had no bearing on the story. The one who liked it felt that the violent scenes were important parts of the story.

Then the friend who didn't like the movie claimed that it was a foregone conclusion that violence in the media affected children and that Hollywood should be held accountable for what it caused. They finally agreed to disagree and decided to get a cup of coffee.

Lesson 9

A daughter who had been studying in another country for a year just returned home and had a conversation with her father. The problem was, she just wanted to go to bed because she had jet lag. Wanting to keep her awake because it was the middle of the afternoon, her father suggested that they take a walk. He thought that she might get a second wind from taking a walk and getting some fresh air.

On the walk, they talked about how they had missed each other. The daughter described her ups and downs while she was away, and explained that holidays were the hardest times for her. She had been homesick a lot. But when spring came, she said it hit home that she was very lucky to have the opportunity to study abroad, and she started to get out of her rut. She ended up having a great time.

Lesson 10

Two people were having lunch at a restaurant. The woman was complaining about her new boss, who was very unpleasant and who gave her too much work. She explained that when she went to talk to her boss about all the work, her boss talked so much, she couldn't get a word in edgewise.

A few minutes later, the woman at the table saw her boss pass by. She realized that her boss had heard everything, and she wanted to go through the floor. She said she had put her foot in her mouth, and would never live this down. Her friend told her that it was over and done with, and that when she went back to the office she would be able to straighten things out.

Walk and Talk Forms for Exercise 5

- Put the names of the students you talk to in the spaces on the left.

- Ask each person no more than two questions. Then move on to someone else.

- Don't ask the same question more than once.

- Write very short notes in the spaces after each question. Do not write full sentences. Write just enough so you remember what your partners said. As you write, try to frequently look up at the person you are talking to.

- After you have completed this activity, you might want to write what your classmates said on a separate sheet of paper. As you write, be sure to include the new expressions in your sentences. To check what you have written, you can *Walk and Talk* again and show your writing to the students you interviewed.

Lesson 1, page 13

_____ 1. Are you the kind of person who keeps things that bother you bottled up inside, or do you get things off your chest? Explain, and give some examples.

_____ 2. What are two activities or sports that scare you? Why don't you have the guts to do those things?

_____ 3. What is something that you wouldn't be caught dead doing? Who is someone that you wouldn't want to be caught dead with? Name a place where you wouldn't be caught dead. Give your reasons.

_____ 4. Have you ever bitten off more than you could chew? Describe what happened.

_____ 5. Do you generally do things on time, or do you put things off? Explain by giving some examples.

_____ 6. What are some things that people do that put you off?

_____ 7. Have you ever hit it off with anyone immediately? Explain the circumstances.

_____ 8. What is life bound to be like in the 21st century?

_____ 9. What is one kind of food that you can never pass up?

_____ 10. What are two ways students can take the initiative to speak to native speakers of English?

Lesson 2, page 32

_____ 1. Is there anyone in your family that you don't particularly like? If yes, what is it about his or her personality that rubs you the wrong way?

_____ 2. Who did you look up to as a child, and why?

_____ 3. In your native culture, what types of behavior are looked down on?

_____ 4. Think about something you did in the past (getting married, moving to a certain place, picking this place to study English, voting for a particular candidate in an election). Now, in hindsight, did you make the right decision? Explain.

_____ 5. List three things that you can do without and three things that you can't do without.

_____ 6. Can you think of a situation in which someone said something critical about you or asked you a personal question and you were very taken aback? What did you do?

_____ 7. Is there anything that you are fed up with right now? Explain.

Lesson 3, page 52

_____ 1. What are two or three things that bore you to death?

_____ 2. Think of a situation that you hated being in (perhaps a party, a wedding, a trip, a show, etc.). Did you stick it out to the end? Why or why not?

_____ 3. Which subjects that you have studied in school sparked your interest? Which didn't spark your interest?

_____ 4. What is something that you do only once in a blue moon? Why?

_____ 5. What kind of food do you like an awful lot? What kind of people do you like an awful lot? Why?

_____ 6. In what situations do you often find your mind wandering?

_____ 7. Everyone has had the experience of being on the edge of their seats at some kind of show, movie, or other type of performance. Describe one experience that you have had.

_____ 8. On vacation, when you have time to just fool around, what do you like to do?

_____ 9. Have you ever bombed a test? If yes, explain the circumstances.

Lesson 4, page 69

_____ 1. Is there a minimum wage in your native country? Is it enough for people to live on?

_____ 2. Certain things and people live on even after their time has passed. For example, John Lennon of the Beatles was killed, but his music lives on. What other people or things live on and on?

_____ 3. Is it common for people you know to live from paycheck to paycheck, or do they actually save money?

_____ 4. Think of a relative of yours who has passed away (died). What is something happening today (personal, political, or social) that might cause that person to turn over in his or her grave?

_____ 5. As a student, do you generally keep up with your work, or do you always feel you are trying to catch up?

_____ 6. Have you ever had a teacher or boss who really piled on the work? If yes, how did you handle it?

_____ 7. If you were a teacher or boss, would you pile work on your students or employees? Explain.

_____ 8. What does a person need to do to move up the ladder in your native country? Are the opportunities to move up the same for men and women? Explain.

_____ 9. Do you know anyone who has worked too much day in and day out and then gotten burned out? If yes, explain the situation.

Lesson 5, page 90

_____ 1. What is Michael's mother (in Exercise 2) worried about? Reread her letter and make a list of her concerns about his sudden wealth. Add any concerns that you might have.

_____ 2. Think of a friend or relative whose behavior seemed to suddenly change (becoming very happy or depressed) Did you say something to anyone equivalent to the expression "What's gotten into him/her?" Explain the circumstances.

_____ 3. What are some American customs that are unheard of in your native country? What are some customs in your native country that are unheard of in the U.S.?

_____ 4. Describe some news that you once heard that took time to sink in. (This would be news that was a good or bad shock, that was hard to believe at first.)

_____ 5. Do foreign children ever attend schools in your native country? If yes, are they given language classes, or are they expected to enter regular classes and "sink or swim"?

_____ 6. Complete these three sentences with the expression *let alone:*

    a) I can't _____ , let alone _____ .

    b) It's difficult to _____ , let alone _____ .

    c) I don't want to _____ , let alone _____ .

_____ 7. What do you think is in store for you after you finish studying English?

_____ 8. What aspects of your life are up in the air?

_____ 9. Describe a time when your efforts to do something went down the drain.

_____ 10. Describe the life of someone (real or imaginary) who's got it made.

Lesson 6, page 107

_____ 1. What are three to five events that can happen out of the blue and surprise people? Make a list.

_____ 2. Are people in your native country generally better off or worse off financially than they were twenty or thirty years ago? Explain.

_____ 3. When people don't have enough money to buy a lot of things, what are some things they do to "make do"?

_____ 4. Have you ever been cooped up in a car, train, bus, plane, or boat for a long trip? If yes, describe how you (and the others) felt and what you did to pass the time.

_____ 5. What are some kinds of work that you have knocked yourself out doing?

Lesson 7, page 130

_____ 1. What are some things that you took for granted when you were a child?

_____ 2. Because of progress in technology, many medical procedures have taken a quantum leap over what they were years ago. List two or three medical techniques that were unheard of twenty years ago.

_____ 3. What do you have to grapple with the most as you study English: grammar, writing, reading, listening, speaking, pronunciation, general vocabulary, or idioms? Why? And which is the easiest for you?

_____ 4. There are some things that none of us like to do at home or at work. When do you drag your feet because you don't want to do something?

_____ 5. What do you prefer? Complete the following:

I'd take _____ over _____ any day.

I'd take _____ over _____ any day.

I'd take _____ over _____ any day.

_____ 6. What is something that you'd like to do now, but you are holding off for a while? Why are you waiting?

_____ 7. Explain ways politicians try to win people over with their speeches.

_____ 8. What are you apt to be doing in ten years?

Lesson 8, page 148

_____ 1. Think about something that disappointed you—a trip, a movie, a restaurant, a course, etc. Then explain why it left a lot to be desired.

_____ 2. When you were a child, did your parents let you get away with murder, or were they strict? Explain.

_____ 3. From your standpoint, how should parents discipline their children—with words or by striking them physically?

_____ 4. The news media are often accused of blowing stories out of proportion. In other words, they may take a story and make it sound more important than it really is. What do you think? (If possible, give examples from the news.)

_____ 5. Explain two or three things that you have yet to do (things that you should have already done long ago).

_____ 6. Give an example of a bone of contention between you and a friend or relative. Or, if you'd rather not get too personal, give an example of a bone of contention between two politicians with different beliefs.

_____ 7. What is the most expensive thing you bought during this past year? Did you get your money's worth? Explain.

_____ 8. What drives you up the wall at home? At school? At work? In this country?

Lesson 9, page 169

_____ 1. Have you ever had jet lag? If yes, where were you? What did you do to stay awake? If you were awake when everyone else was sleeping, what did you do?

_____ 2. Describe a time when you were so wiped out that you couldn't keep your eyes open. Also explain whether or not you got a second wind.

_____ 3. If you are living in a foreign culture, or if you have ever lived in a foreign culture, describe some of the ups and downs that you have experienced.

_____ 4. If you cook, do you generally prefer to make things from scratch or to buy items that make your work easier? Explain. (An example would be a cake mix. With a mix, you could bake a cake very easily and quickly, but if you bake a cake from scratch, you would have to supply all the ingredients.)

_____ 5. What is something that you can get completely wrapped up in? Explain. (Possibilities include work, a good book, your family, political issues.)

_____ 6. What are some kinds of decisions that you would not want to make very quickly? In other words, when might you say, "I can't make that decision now. I have to sleep on it"?

Lesson 10, page 187

_____ 1. Although it may be painful, try to think of a time when you wanted to go through the floor. What happened?

_____ 2. Is there anyone in your family who talks so much that you can't get a word in edgewise? If yes, how do you handle this person?

_____ 3. Describe a time when your plans to do something got fouled up.

_____ 4. What kind of behavior gets to you?

_____ 5. What is something that you could kick yourself for doing?

_____ 6. What do you think is the best way for people who have had a disagreement to straighten things out?

Directions for Two-Word Verb Contact Assignments for Exercise 11*

It would be a good idea, at least at first, if you do Exercise 11 with a partner. If you are prepared and know what to say when you approach someone, you will most likely have a very positive experience.

Here are the guidelines you should follow:

1. Find out where you can find people to talk to. You might approach people at school, at a local store or library, or in your neighborhood. This might be your chance to start conversations with people that you see occasionally but don't know well. You do not have to and should not approach complete strangers on the street.
2. Explain to people who you talk to what you are doing and why, and tell them that your questions will be brief. You might want to start by saying something like this:

"Excuse me, I'm from ___ , and I'm studying English. For homework I'm supposed to find out the meanings of some idiomatic expressions, and I wonder if you would mind answering a few questions."

By the way, you might be surprised to find out that most native speakers of English have never heard of the label "two-word verbs," although they use these expressions frequently.

Most people will be happy to answer your questions, especially once they know that you are working on a class assignment. If you have trouble understanding what a person says, don't hesitate to ask for repetition or clarification. Just say, "Could you please repeat that?" or "Could you possibly give me (us) an example?"

---

*Adapted from *Sound Ideas: Advanced Listening and Speaking,* by Fragiadakis and Maurer, Heinle & Heinle Publishers, 1995.

Student Idiom Collection for Exercise 12

Directions:

1. Find three expressions per week outside of class. These expressions may come from:

   - what you hear on TV and the radio and in the movies and general conversation
   - what you read in newspapers, magazines, books, advertisements, and on billboards, signs, T-shirts, bumper stickers, etc.

2. Keep your collection growing, either in your notebook or on 3 x 5 cards.
3. Follow the format indicated below. If you wish, ask others to explain the expressions that you collect. (Refer to Appendix C for how to approach people to answer your questions about English.)
4. If time permits, you may be asked to teach some of the expressions you collect to your classmates.

Expression: _____

Where I heard it: _____

_____

_____

Who said it:
(indicate whether male or female and approximate age)

_____

_____

Sentence with the expression: _____

_____

_____

What I think the expression means: _____

_____

_____

Answer Key

For Exercises 1, 2, and 6
(and Exercise 4 where indicated in particular lessons)

Lesson 1

Exercise 1: Mini-Dialogues

1. A/B

1. e
2. a
3. f
4. d
5. b

2. A/B

1. e
2. a
3. f
4. b
5. d

3. A/B

1. f
2. a
3. b
4. c
5. d

Exercise 2: Choosing the Idiom

1. What's eating you
2. don't have the guts to
3. hit it off
4. wouldn't be caught dead
5. pass up
6. is bound to
7. get off your chest
8. bite the bullet
9. put it off
10. bite my head off
11. Give it a shot
12. That'll be the day

Exercise 4: Pronunciation

PRACTICE 1

	Usually Stressed	Usually Unstressed
Nouns	√	
Pronouns		√
Main Verbs	√	
Verb *be*		√
Affirmative Helping Verbs		√
Negative Helping Verbs	√	
Adjectives	√	
Adverbs	√	
Conjunctions		√
Prepositions		√
Articles		√
This/that/these/those	√	
Wh question words	√	

Exercise 6: Write Your Own (possible answers)

1. You look so unhappy! What's eating you? Come on, tell me what it is. Don't keep it bottled up inside. You know if you tell me what's bothering you, you're bound to feel a lot better.
2. I know you have mixed feelings about moving away. But how can you pass this up? If I were you, I'd give it a shot even though it's bound to be a little difficult in the beginning. Don't tell me you don't have the guts to do this!
3.
A: I have to get something off my chest.
B: What is it?
A: You know, since you got that new job you hardly ever spend time with the family. You're making more money, but I think you've bitten off more than you can chew.
B: No, I haven't. It's a great job, and I'm sure I'll have a lot more time really soon.
A: That'll be the day.

Lesson 2

Exercise 1: Mini-Dialogues

1. A/B
1. c
2. g
3. a
4. d
5. f
6. h
7. b

2. A/B
1. b
2. f
3. g
4. a
5. e
6. c
7. i
8. d

Exercise 2: Choosing the Idiom

1. get up in arms
2. taken aback
3. fed up with
4. let it slide/swallowed my pride
5. looked down on
6. swallowed my pride/could see his point
7. so as not to
8. rubbed me the wrong way
9. The bottom line

Exercise 6: Write Your Own (possible answers)

1. One of my classmates asked to borrow some money from me. I was taken aback because I didn't know him very well, but so as not to hurt his feelings, I lent him $5. (I lent $5 to him.) The next day he paid me back. In hindsight, I shouldn't have worried.
2. I'm really fed up with this traffic. I realize now that I'm not happy living in such a big city, and I can do without all the excitement. The bottom line is health and happiness, isn't it? I'm going to quit my job and move.
3. Why do you keep saying those things? Yesterday I swallowed my pride and let it slide, but not today. Your comments really rub me the wrong way. Why are you so critical of him (her)?

Lesson 3

Exercise 1: Mini-Dialogues

1. A/B
1. d
2. a
3. b
4. f
5. c

2. A/B
1. a
2. f
3. e
4. c
5. b

3. A/B
1. f
2. e
3. a
4. d
5. b

Exercise 2: Choosing the Idiom

1. once in a blue moon
2. bored to death
3. was on the edge of my seat
4. an awful lot
5. buckle down
6. mind was wandering
7. it dawned on
8. stick it out
9. What a drag
10. fooled around

Exercise 6: Write Your Own (possible answers)

1.
A: You know, it just dawned on me that maybe we can help each other out.
B: Oh, really? How?
A: Well, you know that I've been goofing off. I keep bombing my tests, and I know that it's time for me to buckle down. But I need some help.
B: Uh-huh.
A: And I heard that you want to learn the guitar.
B: Uh-huh.
A: So, why don't we teach each other?
B: Good idea. I think I'll take you up on that. When do we start?

2. You wouldn't believe that party. What a drag! I didn't know anyone and I was bored to death. There were an awful lot of people there, and I just couldn't get myself to start talking to anyone. It dawned on me in the middle of that party how much I really love my friends. For me, it comes down to this: if I'm not with my true friends, I'm not happy.
3. You wouldn't believe how scary that movie was! I was on the edge of my seat the whole time. I couldn't breathe. No one could. It was so quiet in the theater, you could hear a pin drop. The movie was so scary that an awful lot of people actually walked out early. They just couldn't stick it out. But I could. I guess it boils down to the fact that I'm pretty brave.

Lesson 4

Exercise 1: Mini-Dialogues

1. A/B

1. d
2. a
3. c
4. e
5. b
6. g
7. h

2. A/B

1. b
2. h
3. a
4. f
5. d
6. e
7. c

Exercise 2: Choosing the Idiom

1. piling on
2. let up
3. keep up
4. in this neck of the woods
5. at stake
6. Day in and day out
7. got burned (burnt) out
8. catch up
9. dead wrong

Exercise 6: Write Your Own (possible answers)

1. What a movie! I really cried. It was about a poor widow with six kids. They lived from hand to mouth. And when they had nothing at all to live on, they went to a soup kitchen in a church. Day in and day out, they suffered. But they were able to get by.
2. I plan to move up the ladder here really fast. I'm going to keep up with my work. I don't plan to blow this opportunity, and I don't think I'll ever get burned out.
3. OK, everyone. Listen to me. If you think this class is going to be easy, that's wishful thinking. If you think I'm an easy grader, you're dead wrong. You're going to work very hard here. I pile on the work every day, and it doesn't let up until final exams are over. Now, don't let me down. Work hard. I know you can do it.

Lesson 5

Exercise 1: Mini-Dialogues

1. A/B

1. d
2. a
3. e
4. b
5. f

2. A/B

1. b
2. f
3. a
4. d
5. c

3. A/B

1. a
2. e
3. b
4. d
5. c

Exercise 2: Choosing the Idiom

1. sink in
2. to say the least
3. let alone
4. have (got) it made
5. have a sinking feeling
6. be on the lookout
7. go down the drain
8. unheard of
9. make the most of
10. beyond the shadow of a doubt
11. are up in the air
12. is in store

Exercise 6: Write Your Own (possible answers)

1.
A: I can't believe she really won! It's beyond my comprehension!
B: I can't believe it either. It'll take time to sink in.
A: I wonder what's in store for her in the future. Maybe she'll be the first woman President!
B: Who knows?

2. You know, I just went to work that day, as usual. I didn't have the slightest idea that my whole life was going to change. But when I walked into the quiet office and saw that white envelope on my desk, my heart sank. I immediately thought my career was going to go down the drain. When I finally opened the envelope and read the bad news, I put my head in my hands. My whole life was up in the air again, after I had tried so hard. But I'm better now. I'm on the lookout for a really good job, and I even have a few interviews next week.

3. What's gotten into you? You're selling *everything*? That's unheard of. You're crazy, to say the least. I can't believe what's happening, let alone help you sell your stuff. But I've got to hand it to you—you've got guts (courage)!

Lesson 6

Exercise 1: Mini-Dialogues

1. A/B
1. f
2. d
3. c
4. a
5. b
6. g

2. A/B
1. c
2. b
3. d
4. f
5. a
6. e

Exercise 2: Choosing the Idiom

1. cooped up
2. climb the walls
3. sit tight
4. am at the end of my rope
5. knocking herself out
6. kept a level head
7. come through

Exercise 6: Write Your Own (possible answers)

1. I hate being cooped up in here. I'm climbing the walls. We'd be better off at home than sitting here. But I guess we have to make do. We have no choice. Does anyone want to play a game?

2. You know, I got a letter out of the blue from an old friend of mine from high school. We haven't been in touch in years, and apparently he knocked himself out trying to track me down. He finally got my address

from my brother. Well, anyway, he remembered that we had stopped talking to each other because of a big argument, and he said that it was no use crying over spilt milk. He wants to see me but doesn't want to dwell on the past. I guess in the old days we were really good friends, but that fight we had was pretty bad. Anyway, I'm going to see him next week. It should be interesting.

3. Well, that's the last straw. Out of the corner of my eye I could see one of you copy from another, and to tell you the truth, cheating in this class has gotten out of hand. Really, I'm at the end of my rope. I've tried to warn you, but some of you just won't listen.

Lesson 7

Exercise 1: Mini-Dialogues

1. A/B

1. e
2. g
3. a
4. d
5. c
6. b

2. A/B

1. d
2. b
3. g
4. a
5. f
6. c

Exercise 2: Choosing the Idiom

1. are online
2. a quantum leap
3. held off
4. at home
5. tear him away
6. will take
7. drag his feet
8. grappling with
9. plugged away
10. win us over

Exercise 4: Pronunciation

PRACTICE 1

1. z
2. z
3. z
4. z
5. z
6. z
7. z
8. z
9. z
10. z
11. s
12. z
13. ɪz
14. z
15. s
16. z
17. s, z, s

PRACTICE 2

1. s	9. z
2. z	10. z
3. s	11. s
4. ɪ/ɪz	12. z
5. z	13. z
6. z	14. z
7. s	15. z
8. s	

PRACTICE 3

/s/   /z/
Two *parents* ‿ are talking to each other about their young *daughter's* ‿
                                        /s/
ability to use a computer. The father *points* ‿ out that she isn't afraid of
                                              /z/   /z/
technology because she has grown up with *VCRs*, answering *machines*,
          /z/   /z/   /s/
cordless *phones* ‿ and computer *games*. The mother *suggests* that they get
                                        /ɪz/
a babysitter and start computer *classes*.
                              /ɪz/
    After they start their *classes*, they use their computer more. In fact, the
          /z/
father *plugs* ‿ away at the computer every day. He's happy to have a
              /z/   /z/   /z/
teacher who *explains things* to him. His wife *agrees* because she doesn't like
                        /z/
to read computer *manuals*. She is so enthusiastic about using a computer
          /s/   /z/
that she *wants* to buy a modem so they can get online. It *sounds* like everyone
              /z/   /z/
in this family *knows* more about *computers* ‿ every day.

Exercise 6: Write Your Own (possible answers)

1. There are no ifs, ands, or buts about it. I dragged my feet for too long, and I'm going to buy a good computer. I really want to be online. It will help me when I do research. And I need a computer to type my papers. Computers are a quantum leap over old-fashioned typewriters because it's so easy to make corrections on them.

2. Oh, my children take it for granted that I will do everything for them. I shop, cook and clean, drive them everywhere, and help them grapple with their problems. But now that they're getting older, things are going to change. They will have to tear themselves away from their friends and do more around the house. They need to know that it is their responsibility to help out around here.

3.

Child: Daddy, please can I keep the puppy? Look at him—he's so cute.

Father: Dogs are so much work. Why don't we hold off for a while, and look for a nice cat?

Child: But look at him. He'll grow on you, I know it. Look at his eyes. He's looking at you. I'll take him over a cat any day.

Father: He's apt to be a lot of trouble, but it's true, he has very sweet eyes. Oh, well, I guess you won me over. You can keep him. But you'll also have to take care of him.

Lesson 8

Exercise 1: Mini-Dialogues

1. A/B
1. d
2. a
3. b
4. c
5. e

2. A/B
1. f
2. d
3. e
4. b
5. g
6. c

Exercise 2: Choosing the Idiom

1. a bone of contention
2. drove me up the wall
3. nothing to write home about
4. from my standpoint
5. It's not written in stone
6. doesn't hold water
7. have yet to
8. get through to
9. blowing (the value of a computer) out of proportion

Exercise 4: Pronunciation

PRACTICE 1

1. t
2. d
3. ɪd
4. ɪd
5. d
6. d
7. t
8. ɪd
9. d
10. d
11. ɪd
12. d
13. ɪd
14. t
15. d
16. ɪd

PRACTICE 2

Two people went to a violent movie. One of them *liked*⁀ /t/ it a lot, and the other *hated*⁀ /ɪd/ it. The movie *showed*⁀ /d/ a lot of blood and killing, and it *ended* /ɪd/ with probably a hundred people dead. Of course, the person who *disliked* /t/ the movie *wanted* /ɪd/ to leave as soon as it *started,* /ɪd/ but he *agreed* /d/ to stay because his friend *wanted* /ɪd/ to stay.

After the movie they *talked* /t/ for at least an hour. The guy *claimed* /d/ that all that violence *affected* /ɪd/ the way children *behaved,* /d/ and gave them examples of how people *committed* /ɪd/ crimes. His friend *listened* /d/ and said she *hoped* /t/ he was wrong.

Exercise 6: Write Your Own (possible answers)

1.

A: How was your vacation?

B: Not so great. It left a lot to be desired.

A: I'm sorry. What happened?

B: Well, when we got there, we were disappointed in the hotel. Believe me, it was nothing to write home about. The information we received wasn't true at all. The swimming pool had no water, and the room was nothing special. And the people in the room above us made so much noise that they drove us up the wall.

A: That sounds terrible. How long did you stay there?

B: Just one night. Then we switched to a better hotel. I told the manager at the first hotel that from my standpoint their advertising wasn't accurate and that we were going to leave.

2.

Dear Mom and Dad,

All my life it's been a foregone conclusion that I would go to college. But now that I'm graduating from high school, I realize that my future is not written in stone. I don't want to go to college next year. I want to get a job and maybe go to college later. I know this is going to be a bone of contention with you, but please understand. I've made up my mind. I hope you respect my decision.

Lesson 9

Exercise 1: Mini-Dialogues

1. A/B
1. e
2. a
3. f
4. d
5. c
6. g

2. A/B
1. f
2. a
3. c
4. g
5. e
6. d

Exercise 2: Choosing the Idiom

1. wiped out
2. get over jet lag
3. hopped on
4. am all ears
5. scratch the surface
6. are getting a second wind
7. it hit home
8. had my ups and downs
9. wrapped up in

Exercise 6: Write Your Own (possible answers)

1. I have so much to study, and I haven't even scratched the surface yet! What am I going to do? I'm so wiped out, I can't keep my eyes open. Maybe I should stretch out for a few minutes. If I rest a bit, maybe I'll get a second wind.

2.
A: Can I talk to you about my job?
B: Sure. I'm all ears.
A: Well, the job is really boring, and I feel like I'm in a rut. I'm not learning anything new. I want to look for another job.
B: Do you want my advice? Don't do anything you'll be sorry for later. Sleep on it before you tell your boss you're quitting.
A: Thanks. That's good advice.

3.
A: Dad, I broached the subject before and you didn't want me to bring it up again, but I have to. I'm moving to an apartment with two of my friends. It's a great place—it's not expensive, it's in a good neighborhood, and to top that off, it's very close to the college.
B: Can't you stay home where you belong? What's wrong with living here?
A: Nothing. But I'm eighteen now, and I think I'm ready to live on my own. Can you just please mull it over for a while? You'll eventually see that it's a good idea. And I'll come visit you and Mom a lot, I promise.

Lesson 10

Exercise 1: Mini-Dialogues

1. A/B

1. e
2. d
3. a
4. f
5. c

2. A/B

1. a
2. f
3. b
4. e
5. c

Exercise 2: Choosing the Idiom

1. put my foot in my mouth
2. I will never live this down
3. get a word in edgewise
4. straighten things out
5. under the impression
6. hold a grudge against
7. for a good

Exercise 6: Write Your Own (possible answers)

1. Last night I did a terrible thing. I was telling jokes about men with toupees, when a guy took his toupee off right in front of me! I was so embarrassed, I wanted to go through the floor. I could have kicked myself. I really put my foot in my mouth, that's for sure.
2. I've been working on your assignment for a good two weeks, and I want to do a good job. But I've been so busy with work and have been trying in vain to meet your deadline. But I'm not ready. I fouled up. Can you give me an extension?
3. I'm really upset. This is the second afternoon that I've stayed home waiting for someone to fix the sink. Yesterday when I called, they said something had come up, so the guy would come today instead. But I've already been waiting for three hours, and this is really getting to me. I'm going to call again and try to straighten things out.

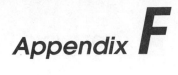

Appendix F

Crossword Puzzle Solution Lessons 1 & 2

				¹B											
		²O		I		³I									
⁴S	⁵I	N	I	T	I	A	T	I	V	E	⁶	⁷C	H	E	S	⁸T
⁹O	U	T						A		A				¹⁰O	F	F
		¹¹H	I	N	D	¹²S	I	G	H	T		U		N		
						W		I		G		N		G		
				¹³W	A	S		N		H		U				
				L				¹⁴G	U	T	¹⁵S		E			
¹⁶S	K	I	P	¹⁷		L					L					
			O	¹⁸S	H	O	T				I					
			I	W		W					D					
			N	A				¹⁹T	H	E						
		²⁰T	A	L	K	I	N	G								
			L				²¹Y									
		²²T	O		²³T	O										
		²⁴W	I	T	H	O	U	T								
			E		R											

Crossword Puzzle Solution Lessons 3 & 4

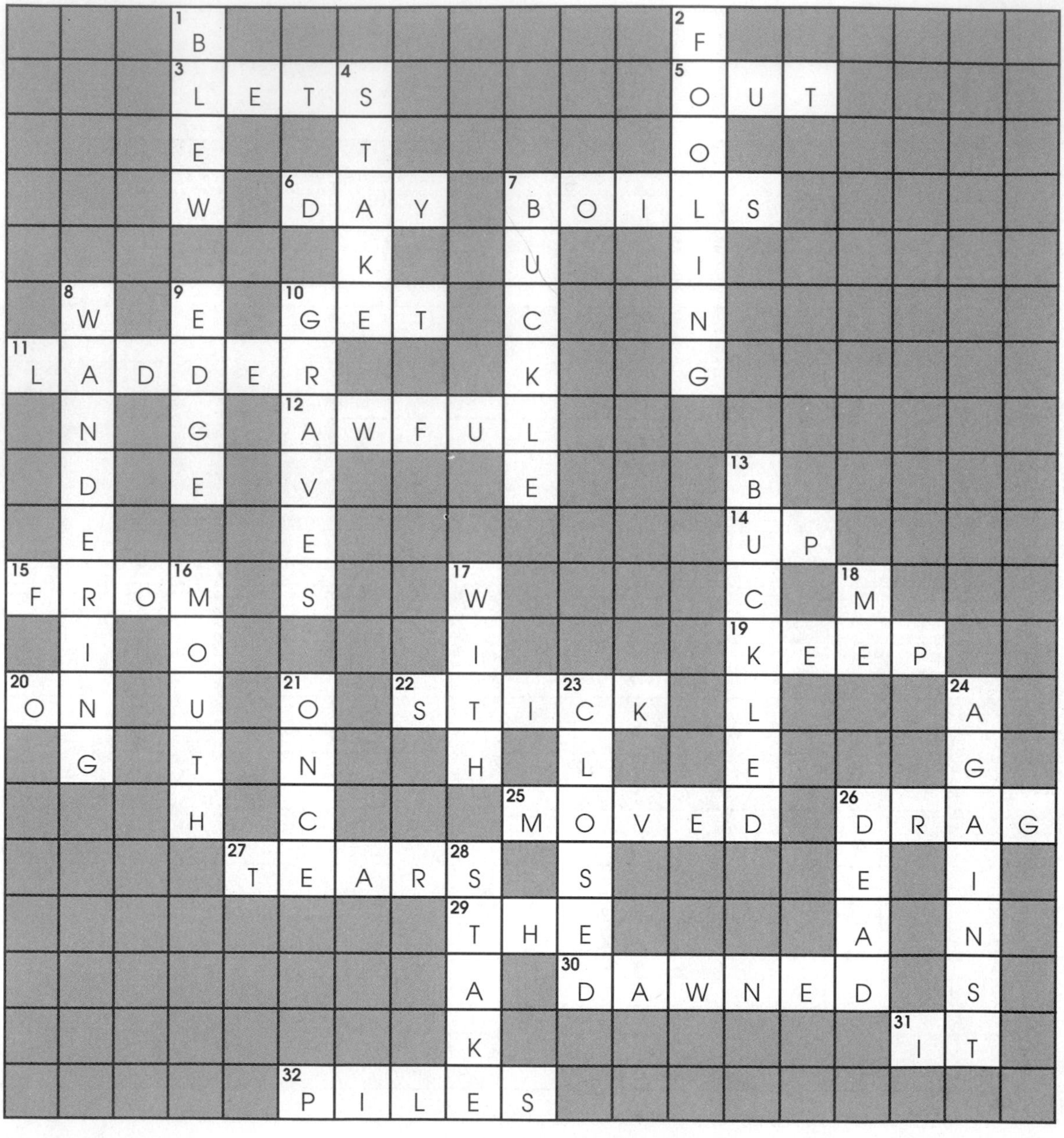

1 BLEW
2 FOOLING
3 LETS
4 STAKE
5 OUT
6 DAY
7 BOILS
7 BUCKLE
8 WANDERING
9 EDGE
10 GET
10 GRAVES
11 LADDER
12 AWFUL
13 BUCKLED
14 UP
15 FROM
16 MOUTH
17 WITH
18 ME
19 KEEP
20 ON
21 ONCE
22 STICK
23 CLOSE
24 AGAINST
25 MOVED
26 DRAG
26 DEAD
27 TEARS
28 STAKE
29 THE
30 DAWNED
31 IT
32 PILES

The crossword solution grid contains the following answers:

Across / Down entries:

- 1. THROUGH
- 2. HIMSELF
- 3. STORE
- 4. ALONE / TALONE
- 5. OFF
- 6. MYSELF
- 7. OUT
- 8. MADE
- 9. DEW / DELL
- 10. CLUE / COOM
- 11. BLUE
- 12. SPILL
- 13. MY / MPL
- 14. OF
- 15. FEEL
- 16. CRYING / CREHEN
- 17. KN
- 18. UP
- 19. BEATS / BLING
- 20. STRAW
- 21. SHADOW
- 22. THE
- 23. GUESS
- 24. SINK
- 25. T
- 26. SLIGHTEST
- 27. HEAD / EATE
- 28. S
- 29. CABIN / CANK
- 30. DRAIN

Crossword Puzzle Solution Lessons 7 & 8

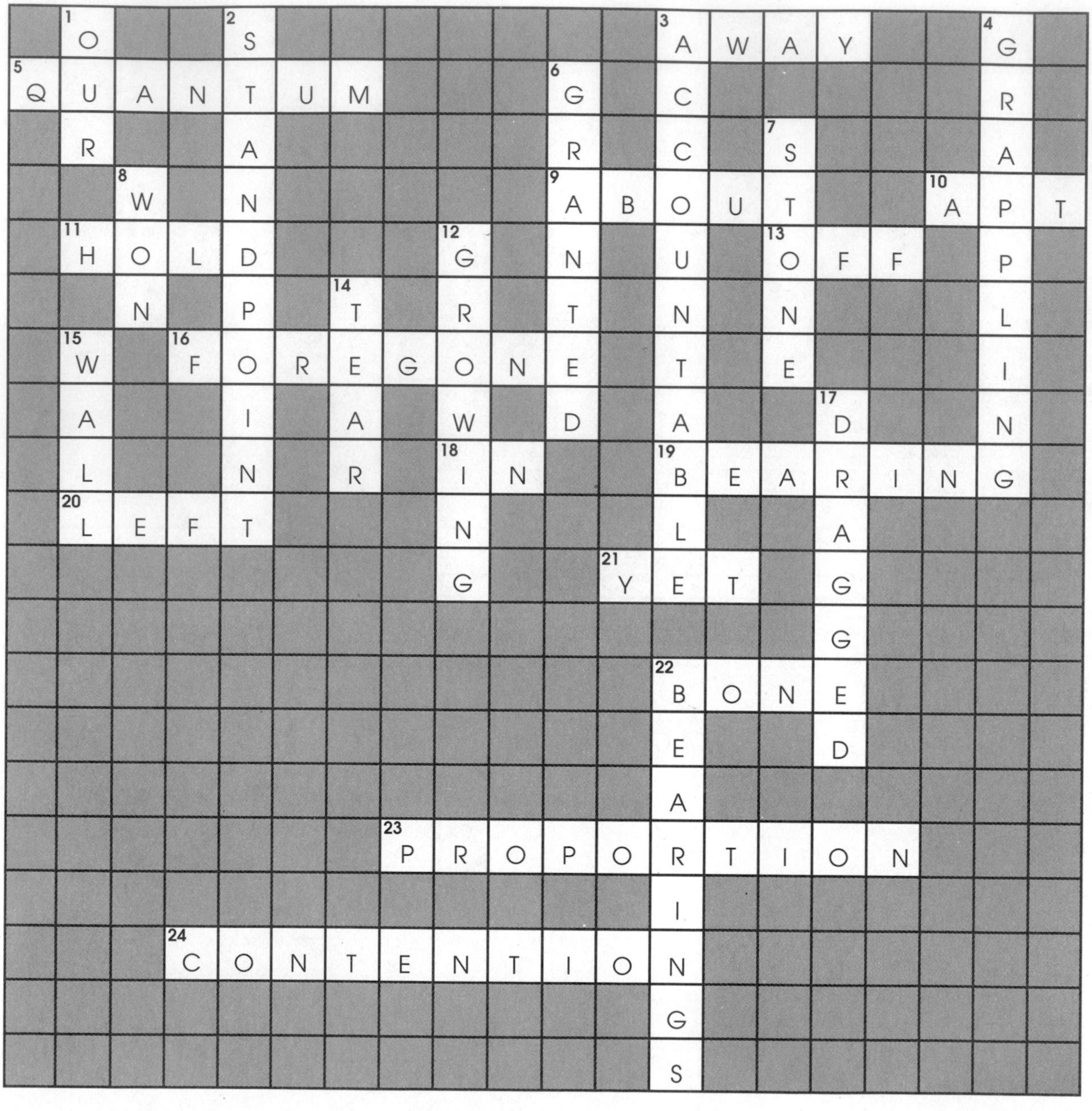

1 OUR
2 STANDPOINT
3 AWAY
3 ACCOUNTABLE
4 GRAPPLING
5 QUANTUM
6 GRANTED
7 STONE
8 WON
9 ABOUT
10 APT
11 HOLD
12 GROWING
13 OFF
14 TEAR
15 WALL
16 FOREGONE
17 DRAGGED
18 IN
19 BEARING
20 LEFT
21 YET
22 BONE
22 BEARINGS
23 PROPORTION
24 CONTENTION

The crossword grid solution contains the following answers:

- 1 Down: A G A I N S T
- 2 Across: B R O U G H T
- 3 Down: R U B
- 4 Across: D O W N S
- 5 Down: S L E E P T
- 6 Across: I T
- 7 Down: I N S
- 8 Across: O N
- 9 Across: W R A P
- 10 Down: W
- 11 Down: H A N T
- 12 Across: S C R A T C H
- 12 Down: S C R A T C H E D
- 13 Down: F U L L
- 14 Across: C O U L D N T
- 15 Across: H O M E
- 16 Down: H U L L
- 17 Across: E D G E W I S E
- 17 Down: E D
- 18 Down: G O T
- 19 Down: I D
- 20 Down: M U S T
- 21 Across: M Y S E L F
- 22 Down: S E E E
- 23 Down: F O O T
- 24 Across: E A R S
- 24 Down: E D
- 25 Down: T R
- 26 Across: S T R A I G H T E N
- 26 Down: S I N
- 27 Across: B R O A C H
- 28 Across: H O P
- 29 Down: G O
- 30 Across: G O O D
- 31 Across: S T R E T C H

Student Self-Evaluation Questionnaire

Name (Optional): _____

Date: _____

It is valuable to occasionally stop and reflect on your learning. Below, circle the number that shows how much you agree or disagree with the statement on the left.

	Disagree Strongly			Agree Strongly	
1. My knowledge of idiomatic expressions has increased.	1	2	3	4	5
2. I occasionally try to use some of these expressions when I speak.	1	2	3	4	5
3. When I listen to native speakers of English, I listen for expressions that I have been studying.	1	2	3	4	5
4. When I see or hear expressions that I don't know, I write them down and ask what they mean.	1	2	3	4	5
5. My general knowledge of pronunciation has expanded.	1	2	3	4	5
6. I consciously try to monitor (listen to and correct) my pronunciation.	1	2	3	4	5
7. When I listen to native speakers of English, whether in person or on TV or in the movies, I actively listen for how they use the pronunciation that we've been studying in class.	1	2	3	4	5
8. I'm working hard both in and out of class.	1	2	3	4	5
9. I find studying with others in and out of class to be helpful.	1	2	3	4	5
10. My confidence in my ability to speak English has increased.	1	2	3	4	5

Questions/Comments?

Student Self-Evaluation— The Train

Where Are You in Our Class?

What number or numbers apply to you?

Why? Please write your reasons on the back of this page.

Guide to Pronunciation Symbols

	VOWELS			CONSONANTS	
Symbol	**Key Word**	**Pronunciation**	**Symbol**	**Key Word**	**Pronunciation**
/ɑ/	hot	/hɑt/	/b/	boy	/bɔɪ/
	far	/fɑr/	/d/	day	/deɪ/
/æ/	cat	/kæt/	/dʒ/	just	/dʒʌst/
/aɪ/	fine	/faɪn/	/f/	face	/feɪs/
/aʊ/	house	/haʊs/	/g/	get	/gɛt/
/ɛ/	bed	/bɛd/	/h/	hat	/hæt/
/eɪ/	name	/neɪm/	/k/	car	/kɑr/
/i/	need	/nid/	/l/	light	/laɪt/
/ɪ/	sit	/sɪt/	/m/	my	/maɪ/
/oʊ/	go	/goʊ/	/n/	nine	/naɪn/
/ʊ/	book	/bʊk/	/ŋ/	sing	/sɪŋ/
/u/	boot	/but/	/p/	pen	/pɛn/
/ɔ/	dog	/dɔg/	/r/	right	/raɪt/
	four	/fɔr/	/s/	see	/si/
/ɔɪ/	toy	/tɔɪ/	/t/	tea	/ti/
/ʌ/	cup	/kʌp/	/tʃ/	cheap	/tʃip/
/ɜr/	bird	/bɜrd/	/v/	vote	/voʊt/
/ə/	about	/əˈbaʊt/	/w/	west	/wɛst/
	after	/ˈæftər/	/y/	yes	/yɛs/
			/z/	zoo	/zu/
			/ð/	they	/ðeɪ/
			/θ/	think	/θɪŋk/
			/ʃ/	shoe	/ʃu/
			/ʒ/	vision	/ˈvɪʒən/

Source: *The Newbury House Dictionary of American English*

Index: Alphabetical List of Idioms and Expressions

(The numbers refer to the lesson numbers in this book.)